PILGRIM THROUGH
THIS
BARREN LAND

By
DAVID MORRIS

GEOFFREY BLES

PILGRIM THROUGH THIS BARREN LAND
is published by
GEOFFREY BLES
59 Brompton Road, London SW3 1DS

ISBN 0 7138 0770 9

© David Morris, 1974

Printed by John Sherratt and Son Ltd,
St. Ann's Press, Park Road, Altrincham, Cheshire WA14 5QQ

To
A. K. M. and R. B. M.

"Hear, ye children, the instruction of a father,
and attend to know understanding.
For I give you good doctrine, forsake ye not
my law.
For I was my father's son, tender and only
beloved in the sight of my mother.
He taught me also, and said unto me, Let
thine heart retain my words; keep my com-
mandments, and live."

Acknowledgements

The author is indebted to the following publishers for permission to quote from these works:

England 1870–1914 by R. C. K. Ensor, by permission of The Clarendon Press, Oxford;

Liverpool by George Chandler, published by B. T. Batsford Ltd;

Welsh Country Upbringing by D. Parry Jones, published by B. T. Batsford Ltd;

Biography of Christmas Evans by Ebrard Rees, published by Kingsgate Press;

Social Change in South West Wales by Brennan, Cooney and Pollins, published by Watts & Co;

My Dear Timothy by Victor Gollancz, published by Victor Gollancz Ltd.

Contents

"Once parents are dead, it is tempting for children to immortalise them: describing them is the directest form of autobiography, the most shameless form of self-justification."

ISABEL QUIGLY

All things bright and beautiful,
All creatures great and small,
All things wise and wonderful,
The Lord God made them all.

Each little flower that opens,
Each little bird that sings,
He made their glowing colours,
He made their tiny wings.

The rich man in his castle,
The poor man at his gate,
God made them high or lowly,
And order'd their estate.

The tall trees in the greenwood,
The meadows where we play,
The rushes by the water,
We gather every day:—

He gave us eyes to see them,
And lips that we might tell,
How great is God Almighty,
Who has made all things well.

MRS. ALEXANDER

A*

One

A holiday on a Welsh farm

I have never been back. I am afraid to go. Everyone else is dead. After forty years there would have been too many changes. The present would spoil the remembered past. I am writing this down because I have no brothers or sisters and none of these things exist any longer except in my head. I would like my children to know where they came from before they were born even though I shall never know where they go to after I am dead.

The farm house, cowsheds and stables formed three sides of a square. The house itself was whitewashed with walls two or three feet thick. Over the door was something in black—I can't quite remember what but it was supposed to be something to do with King Arthur whose Round Table, a grassy flat topped mound, was hidden in some woods two miles or so across the fields. As you entered the farm yard from the road the house was straight ahead with the cowsheds and stables on your right—on the open side to the left was the field where the pigs were. Also to the left and separate from the house was the only lavatory—with a scrubbed wooden seat which was very different from the smooth polished seat at home, and the whole smell of going to the lavatory was different—through the door came the smell of the farm yard, and the hot smell of sun on wood and the smell I made myself was different because there was no water and the smell of the bits of newspaper. To the right of the house were the haystacks which I was allowed to climb on and slide and jump off. It was marvellous except for the grass snakes because I was never quite sure they were grass snakes but the earwigs were worse because if one got in your ear you might never get him out again.

The kitchen was the biggest room in the house and we ate there. The bread was baked in an oven in one of the walls and the salt butter was churned in the dairy. Sometimes I helped for a minute or two to churn the butter but that game soon tired—it was too much like hard work—but the butter was so good we had it sent to us at home for years afterwards. I don't remember much about the food apart from the butter and I usually remember about food.

I liked watching the milking—the smell of the cows and the rhythmic pish and ping of the milk in the bucket and one of the men or girls milking squirted some in my face. Apart from the cows, chickens, pigs and horses I think it must have been mainly a sheep farm. There were lots of sheep about. The men worked them with their dogs—collecting them from field and hillside, driving them along roads bringing them to the sheep dip.

One way the road went to Denbigh, the other way to the village. It was a long walk to the village or so it seemed to me at the time. On the way you passed a place where the road came near to a stream and we often stopped there to skim flat stones across the stream. On the opposite side of the road from the stream was a blacksmith's and a mill. The smell of the mill was wonderful and it was the best place I ever knew for charging around in. In the mill you could go down chutes and land in soft places. I liked watching the blacksmith shoeing the horses, the heat of the forge, the dull red of the shoe, the hiss of hot metal in water, the smell of the horses' hooves. From there on to the village, the sides of the road were quite high banks, grass and stone and wild flowers. I suppose if I'd been brought up in the country I would be able to reel off a long list of wild flowers but I wasn't and I can't; anyhow I wasn't really interested in wild flowers. I was interested in wild strawberries and they grew all along those banks—enough of

them to have a real go at—not just one or two here or
there. It was unbelievable—a free gift of strawberries just
to pick and eat.

If we didn't walk to the village we might drive in my
father's car which was the only motor vehicle around. It
was a Singer with a dicky. The passengers had to get out
and push on some of the hills. It was wonderful going along
sitting between my mother and my father with the hood down,
and I enjoyed riding in the dicky until one day my father
stopped suddenly to avoid another car, swerved up on to the
grass verge and jolted me clear out of the dicky and on to
the road. The next time I was flung out of a car was about
1957 in Gray's Inn—that was a jeep—moral—travel with
a roof over your head.

But the best way to go to the village was with the farmer
in his trap. He and his wife used to go in regularly once, or
maybe twice, a week with butter and eggs for the market.
Sometimes he went without his wife and took me. I'm only
guessing but I should think he was about the same age as
my father—somewhere between forty and forty-five—dark-
haired, dark straggly moustache. I can't describe him but
I would recognise him if I saw him. I don't know why he
went to the village without his wife. I used to just stand
around the village until he had finished whatever it was
he went for and then we drove back. I'm very glad I was
born in time to travel in the dicky of a car, on the top deck
of a bus when it was open and in a horse and trap. Sometimes they put me on the horse bare back and gave me a
switch of hazel cut from the hedgerow. I'd only had donkey
rides on the beach before and this seemed rather high. We
went down the hill towards the river and played around but
there were too many horseflies for me. I liked the horses
but the most interesting thing that happened with horses I
never saw. My mother and I had been out one day and got
back to the farm and there was quite a crowd in the farm
yard—men and women, boys and girls—far more people

than were ever there before or after. They were all watching a horse which was being held in the centre of the farm yard while another horse in one of the stables was making a tremendous fuss—he was sort of snorting and his eyes were all white—when suddenly the horse in the stable was let out and went for the other horse. The horse from the stable looked very wild and angry and just as it was about to attack the other one who looked frightened, my mother took me into the farm house and I never saw what happened and when I asked her what was happening she said that she didn't know but I think she did.

I mustn't give you the impression that I thought it was all wonderful at the time. Too many terrifying things happened for that. I've mentioned the snakes and the earwigs. One day I was sitting on top of a loose wall about half a mile from the farm near the stream. I was by myself—my mother and father had gone off for the day and I'd said I'd rather stay behind—so I was just sitting there and obviously I can't remember now what I was thinking about if I was thinking about anything. Anyhow I was playing about with a loose stone on the top of the wall a few inches away from where I was sitting—just lifting a stone up and putting it back again and then I lifted another stone up and looked underneath it and I went on looking for a few moments and then gleaming in the sun I saw something black and yellow and zig-zaggy about half an inch to three quarters of an inch across. I don't know what it was but as I was looking at it and after I'd been looking at it for quite a few moments I suddenly became almost sure that it was the head of a poisonous snake. I was terrified, I dropped the stone, jumped off the wall and ran all the way back to the farm and I only began to feel safe again when I got there.

Near the village was a large empty house. The gardens had grown wild. We only had a backyard at home and I had never seen such a big garden or a kitchen garden—here the raspberry canes were growing high, tangled up with weeds and briars. You could get into the house. All the rooms were empty. We went there once or twice. Later when a friend of my mother and father came to stay for a while on the farm with us I took her to visit this deserted house.

We went inside and for the first time we went upstairs. The stairs were in an unusual position at one end of the house and as you got to the top of the stairs a long corridor stretched the whole length of the house with rooms opening off it. It was a hot drowsy sort of day and as we got to the top of the stairs there was a funny sort of noise. I can't describe it because I've only heard it once in my life. I'm not sure we noticed all that much at first but as we walked along the corridor the noise gradually got louder. It was a bit like the noise of a waterfall in the distance only more high-pitched. We opened doors and looked inside rooms—nothing—until we opened a door right at the end of the corridor and suddenly the noise was over-powering. I didn't react very quickly but I was quicker than the lady I was with. Once again I ran terrified, ran as hard as I could go—back along the corridor, down the stairs, through the overgrown garden and half way home to the farm. After what seemed a long time the lady caught up with me—she was unhurt and she wasn't cross although I thought she might well have been when I had led her into the room and then just ran away. The room had been swarming with bees.

I also got away from the bull. We all knew that bulls charged anything in red, so it was very careless of my mother to dress me in a red and grey check jersey. Sure enough one day I was in a field and the bull saw my red jersey. Fortunately I saw the bull in good time and realised what was going on in the bull's mind so I got away fairly easily. I was frightened but not terrified and I thought it was rather stupid of my mother.

I got away from the poisonous snake if it was a poisonous snake and I got away from the bees which were bees, and I got away from the bull, but I didn't get away from the wasps.

One afternoon walking across some fields near the farm house I trod on a wasps' nest and was stung by quite a few wasps. It was very painful but they took me home to the farm and my mother made a lot of fuss of me and put stuff on the stings and all was well by next day.

There was always something to do or watch. I spent a good many hours watching the pigs. They had made a filthy mess of their field snouting around in it, rooting at cabbage stalks. I wasn't afraid of the pigs and I liked chivvying them around and making them grunt and then they were so marvellously dirty with dried mud on their backs and the hair shining in the sunlight against the skin. The thing was they were just like pigs, individuals, stinking of pigshit and farm mud, whom I could frighten a bit and chase around and make grunt whereas the sheep were just a group—stupid, frightened of the dogs, always panicking and trying to escape and never succeeding and the noise they made wasn't nearly as good or as varied as the noises the pigs made—the half snuffle as they shuffled about, the fuller grunt and the squeak and then there was the curious disproportion between the size of their bodies and their ridiculous small legs and feet—they would go slowly most of the time snuffling and eating but you could make them scurry quite quickly and squeal.

When I was tired of annoying the pigs I would walk around trying the cowpats. It was very difficult to tell by poking whether they would bear your weight. Sometimes they did and sometimes they didn't—but you could see one more or less round baked a yellowy biscuit shade, crumbling round the edges and you tried it out and in your foot went, through the crust and the dark brown liquid squelched over the edge of your shoes and the sweet smell of cowshit came up and the bluebottles buzzed around. Why does horsedung and cowshit and even pigshit smell fine but not human shit and dog shit? Is it because we and the dogs eat meat or cooked foods?

I don't remember any rain at all. Is that the memory playing its usual trick of sifting out the unpleasant and leaving only the golden false illusion of continual hot sunny days or was the summer of 1927 an unusually fine one? I suppose the meteorological office would have records but I haven't bothered to check because whether or not it was a golden summer that is how I remember it. It must have been hot and dry for the cowpats to get their crust.

Another thing I don't remember is what happened about church on Sundays. My father and mother were very conscientious about going to church on holiday. Even I quite liked going to church on holiday because it was the only time my father was next to me in the pew. Except on holiday he was up there in the pulpit. I liked hearing him sing and he would smile at me.

Anyhow I can't remember going to church on Sundays at all this holiday—perhaps we were excused because all the services were in Welsh which was fine for my father but no good for my mother and me. It's true, or so he said, that he had taught me years before to sing "Land of my Fathers" in Welsh but I had forgotten this and only learnt on this holiday a few useful phrases like "goodday" and "you're a filthy pig".

Later on he wasn't there on Sundays—because he went back home at the weekend to preach leaving my mother and me on the farm—I don't know how long we were there— it may only have been six weeks but it seemed like three months.

From Greenland's icy mountains,
From India's coral strand,
Where Afric's sunny fountains
Roll down their golden sand,
From many an ancient river,
From many a palmy plain,
They call us to deliver
Their land from error's chain.

What though the spicy breezes,
Blow soft o'er Ceylon's Isle,
Though every prospect pleases
And only man is vile,
In vain with lavish kindness
The gifts of God are strown,
The heathen in his blindness
Bows down to wood and stone.

Can we, whose souls are lighted
With wisdom from on high,
Can we to men benighted
The lamp of life deny?
Salvation! oh, salvation!
The joyful sound proclaim,
Till each remotest nation
Has learn'd Messiah's name.

Waft, waft, ye winds, His story,
And you, ye waters, roll,
Till, like a sea of glory,
It spreads from pole to pole;
Till oer our ransom'd nature
The Lamb for sinners slain,
Redeemer, King, Creator,
In bliss returns to reign.

BISHOP HEBER

Two

From slavery to salvation in Liverpool

I am a fat, balding, middle-aged commuter. As I look at my reflection in the train windows I see that I have four eyes and that my face lurches and sags like a Francis Bacon painting. It does not seem very likely that I was once invited to a party by Lord Derby and went dressed as a fairy, complete with wand and wings.

The party was in the early twenties and Lord Derby was Lord Mayor of Liverpool. Besides me, he also invited several hundred other young people and children. It was one of the most enjoyable parties I have ever been to. The food was excellent, there was a conjuror, we were allowed to play hide-and-seek all over the building and, when all else palled, we charged in gangs across the ballroom cheerfully ruining the Sir Roger de Coverleys of the sedate teenagers. Several hours later I emerged to be collected by my mother with wings bludgeoned but head unbowed.

The party was held in the Town Hall which was opened in 1754. The same building was also the new Exchange. Its frieze was decorated with negro heads. Four years earlier London's monopoly of the Guinea trade had been broken and the Liverpool merchants had begun their exploitation of the triangular voyage which took a year or more between the West Africa Coast, the West Indies and home, which was to make Liverpool the second port in the kingdom and vastly increase its wealth.

The three-way trade consisted of selling goods cheaply in Africa, buying black men and women and boys and girls and selling them in the West Indies and sailing home with a cargo of sugar and rum. For the merchant and his crew it was a risky business. The ship might be sunk by perils of the sea or captured by a foreign pirateer; the crew could be killed off by disease on the African coast or by shortage of food and water if the middle passage was unexpectedly prolonged. It was a slightly more risky business for the black cargo.

Out of a total of between six and seven hundred slaves carried on a 235-ton Liverpool slave-ship from Bonny, fifteen died before the ship left Bonny river and three hundred during the middle passage. On other occasions one hundred and five negroes out of a cargo of three hundred and eighty died of dysentry; half a cargo of one hundred and five died from lack of food and water and seasickness; one hundred and twenty three died out of a total of one hundred and sixty eight; one fifth of a cargo died from measles; one hundred slaves died "due to bad weather and consequent shortage of food and water"; out of a cargo of four hundred and forty slaves, sixty died and one hundred and thirty two were flung overboard still alive.

These examples are given by Averil Mackenzie Grieve in her book "The Last Years of the English Slave Trade— Liverpool 1750–1807". In another book by George Chandler which was published in 1957 and is described as having been "sponsored by Liverpool City Council to celebrate the 750th Anniversary of Liverpool's first charter" the benefits of the slave trade are described as follows:—

"Africa was hungry for the industrial goods created in England as a result of the Industrial Revolution. The New World needed manual workers available in Africa while England hungered for sugar and tobacco from the New World. In the long run, the triangular operation based on Liverpool was to bring benefits to all, not least to the transplanted slaves, whose descendants have subsequently achieved in the New World standards of education and civilisation far ahead of their compatriots whom they left behind."

I prefer the language of Gomer Williams, writing in 1897 of the trade which made Liverpool great.

"For a period of 77 years they (the Liverpool adventurers) carried on the trade with a characteristic vigour and ability that outdistanced every competitor, and won for Liverpool the unenviable distinction of being the chief slaving town of the Old World."

And speaking of the moral condition of Liverpool in the eighteenth century Gomer Williams said that it was such that privateering was "more likely to elevate than lower the people . . . and that the standard of morality was so low in Liverpool, that even the introduction of piracy itself into the Mersey, as a fine art, would not have perceptively altered the manners and morals of the masses during the first half of the eighteenth century."

Between 1700 and 1800 the population of Liverpool multiplied more than tenfold. In the year 1771 alone according to Averil Mackenzie Grieve "Liverpool ships transported from Africa and sold in the West Indies 28,200 negroes."

When the slave trade was ended in 1807 the port's prosperity continued to depend on slavery—it lived on the imports of cotton from the slave plantations of the American South and the exports of the cheap manufactured cotton goods to India—a trade which at one and the same time involved the exploitatation of black slave labour in the U.S.A., white industrial workers in Lancashire and the brown peasants of India, where the indigenous domestic industry was destroyed never to be revived save as a dream of Gandhi.

With the increasing prosperity of Liverpool came the public buildings, the slums and the churches for a population drawn from all over the world but in particular with an unusually large proportion of immigrants from Ireland and Wales. As the city spread new churches were built and old ones sold off. On the tenth of January 1844 a new Baptist Church was "opened for divine worship" in Myrtle Street. It stood on a ridge between the present Roman Catholic Cathedral and the Philharmonic Hall and not far from the Anglican Cathedral. A few yards down the hill was Rodney Street— later the Harley Street of Liverpool. The street had been named after Admiral Lord Rodney by the grateful Liverpool merchants for his championship of the Slave Trade. And in Rodney Street in 1809 was born William Ewart Gladstone whose father left him a fortune derived in part from a West Indian business based on slavery. Sir John Gladstone owned large plantations in Demerara and elsewhere and in the long struggle for the abolition of the slave trade always spoke up for the interests of the slave-owning planters. In 1830 he published in the form of a letter to Sir Robert Peel a pamphlet in which he argued that the abolition of slavery would be against the interests of the negroes as well as the planters.

On the 3rd June 1833 the son made his first substantial speech in the House of Commons. An attack had been made on the conduct of his father's plantation in Demerara where it was alleged that there was undue mortality among the slaves. Gladstone insisted that they were happy, healthy and contented and although he did not support the principle of slavery he was in favour of only gradual emancipation with full compensation to the owners. Ultimately his father received £93,526 compensation for 2,439 slaves and it has been reckoned that he lost over £125,000 as a result of emancipation.

The new church at Myrtle Street had a past before it opened. In July 1800 some members from Byrom Street Church had formed a Church in Church Lane. In October 1803 the church moved to Lime Street only to be demolished for town improvements in January 1844. Myrtle Street was in the Victorian Gothic style. Side galleries were added in 1851 and it was enlarged in 1859. The membership grew. Daughter churches and missions sprang up. On the 1st January 1848 Hugh Stowell Brown had become its minister. Thirty years later he was President of the Baptist Union. During those years he had joined that select group of preachers who, during Victoria's reign, acquired the fame, reputation and prestige which in more recent years has been achieved only by pop singers and soccer stars. Some of these preachers also gained a degree of middle-class wealth which put them a world apart from most of their contemporary citizens.

Hugh Stowell Brown was born in 1823 a son of a Church of England Minister in the Isle of Man. His brother T. E. Brown who was well known and well regarded in his lifetime has posthumously won unenviable distinction as the creator and founder of the "God Wottery" school of poetry—he certainly wrote one of the most memorable lines of English verse—

"A garden is a lovesome thing, God wot!"

He was also a schoolmaster and amongst those he influenced was W. E. Henley to whom one of his poems is addressed.

Hugh Stowell Brown himself started off in life as a surveyor's assistant and later worked on the railways. He joined the Baptist denomination at the age of twenty four years and twelve weeks later had been invited to become the Minister of Myrtle Street Baptist Church. He remained its Minister until his death in 1886. In addition to his success as a minister and preacher he also acquired fame as a lecturer to working men on Sunday afternoons. Even nearly a hundred years after his death and in cold print some of the humour and honesty, the blunt appeal of the man still comes through. He could laugh at himself as well as others.

"Evening discourse on *Te Deum*. Seldom seen a fuller congregation. B— before service in a most bewildered state of mind, thought *Te Deum* was some heathen God. After service seemed to think same. Indeed, I fancy many present had never heard of it, and would infinitely prefer a Sankey rhyme."

Describing the end of one of his lectures he wrote:—

" 'Ladies and Gentlemen,' said the mover of thanks to the chairman after one of my poor efforts,—'Ladies and Gentlemen, I call upon you to express your cordial thanks to our excellent chairman for making such a great sacrifice of his time as to come and listen to this lecture.' I have never heard a louder burst of applause than that which followed the proposal."

"On another occasion the bill-stickers served me very shamefully. Some years ago there came from America an enormous cheese, about the size of a hogshead, and it was carried round the country as a show. I and the cheese were unfortunately in a certain town at the same time and so came into competition. The bill announcing my lecture was quite correct in itself, but I observed that, in several instances, the Yankee in charge of the cheese had contrived to injure me. Over my lecture bill he had pasted his announcement, leaving, however, the top line in view, and so it ran—

> "MR. HUGH STOWELL BROWN
> THE BIGGEST CHEESE IN ENGLAND
> WILL BE EXHIBITED
> TONIGHT
> AT THE SPOTTED DOG, CROOKED LANE,
> ADMISSION SIXPENCE."

He was in the ministry for thirty years before he became seriously ill for the first time. He recorded his thoughts in a common place book and among them were these:—

"When I was very low and weak I found Atheism rather a temptation, as affording me a lazy escape from all bother, and chiefly the bother of having to live for ever. It is singular how little I felt of the power and beauty of Christianity when at the worst. I find that sickness makes me selfish, and selfish on a mean scale, so that all fine thought and feeling are suspended. The state of one's bowels and appetite are infinitely more thought of than all the great subjects in Religion, Philosophy, Literature or Politics . . . Sickness makes one small in every way. I find I can be most religious when most in health . . . As to preparing for death, and becoming religious while ill, I think it the greatest of all delusions. It is the last thing a sick man will think of; he is far more concerned about the effect of a pill than about the salvation of his soul."

He was certainly no rigid sectarian—

"There are believers, as well as unbelievers, who are heartily sick of denominationalism and of church and chapel tyranny . . . We Protestants differ from Catholics in many respects, and in this amongst others, that while they have one Pope we have thousands. It has often been observed that the most vehement controversialists are the most successful promoters of the doctrines which they themselves oppose; and, perhaps, every sect has had reason to cry out 'save me from my friends' . . . But here are fellows, calling themselves Protestants, who swindle in trade, tell no end of lies, grind those in their employ to the bones, get drunk, set their hearts upon getting and keeping money, allow their children to go to the devil and show them the way, break out into furious passion, and hate their neighbours with all their hearts; and yet, forsooth, because they curse the Pope and howl against the Ritualists, they are Protestants, and the Bible, and the Bible alone, is their religion . . .

"Having the Bible in our hands, we would fain see an end to all doctrinal articles in chapel trust deeds, and liberty accorded to the clergy and people of the Established Church to form independently for themselves their creed and their mode of worship. It is intolerable, absurd, wretched, to be in these matters, tied and bound by those who have been for ages in their graves. And equally objectionable is it to be muzzled by spiteful gossip concerning what is sound and unsound. Let us all give and take more freedom of thought. Let us in fact be, in the true sense of the word, Freethinkers, and not be afraid to call ourselves such."

Perhaps the fact that he joined the Baptists comparatively late in life gave him an uncommon freedom of perspective. He was well aware of the blemishes of Non-conformist life— some are referred to in the passage from which I have just quoted but he could be more direct.

Speaking of a man who was taken ill and gave notice that in all probability his pew would not be required the next quarter he said "I am thankful to say the prediction was fulfilled" or again he wrote:—

"I buried a woman today. There was no mourner but the husband and he seemed very cheerful. I believe that he has reason to be so."

"Ever since I came to Liverpool the great majority of Myrtle Street Chapel have, insofar as any public manifestation to the contrary is concerned, shown that they don't believe in prayer."

"Many specimens of the religious devil might be described, for example the peevish, quarrelsome, pre-eminence loving church member. This sort of devil is often found in dissenting circles . . . when he can make himself of some importance, gather a party, cause a division, and, in a general way, make havoc of the Church."

Time and again this prototype Victorian successful father figure whose bewhiskered chin and black frock coat carved in stone dominated my childhood visits to Church, this famous and successful preacher wrote in secret of his wish to break away from the Church to whose success he had done so much to contribute. He obviously felt stifled by the congregation "Let us," he said, "admit the possibility of our being in error still, and not be over positive in all our beliefs"— words echoing those of Cromwell—"I beseech you, in the bowels of Christ, think it possible you may be mistaken."

He was not surprised that some churches were nearly empty—note that Churches were nearly empty even in Victoria's reign—"Can any man of commonsense wonder at this? the only matter of surprise is that anybody should be stupid enough to submit to such a dull and wearisome ordeal as awaits him there. The people show their good sense and their religiousness rather by forsaking than frequenting such temples of inanity, such ministries of insufferable dullness."

He was aware that the voluntary system made little provision for the poorer districts of the big towns. "It builds handsome and expensive chapels for the upper and middle classes, but leaves the poor and ignorant to go to the dogs and to the devil."

By 1884 nine separate chapels and missions had been started. The number of members when he took over the Ministry was 239 and by 1884 was 849 including the daughter chapels and missions. These are the numbers of actual Church members, not those of congregations which were substantially higher. On the financial side the picture was equally cheerful.

"Without a penny of endowment, or of public help in any shape, this congregation . . . has built and kept in repair a large and worthy edifice, it has found the pastor, and paid him well; the church has made provision for its own poor members, and never suffered them to sink into a state of abject want, and in this way I have no doubt that the rate-payers of Liverpool have been saved during these many years some thousands of pounds. Whatever has been needed to carry on our Sunday and Ragged Schools, our many Mission Halls, our Bible Women's Union, and other institutions connected with the place, has been promptly supplied. I reckon that . . . the congregation has always given in charity an average of £1,000 a year."

Nor was the heathen in his blindness forgotten. Substantial contributions were made to the work of Missions abroad.

After giving up his Sunday afternoon lectures, he writes, "I did not entirely abandon my old practice of delivering addresses to the working people, for I had the pleasure in the summer of speaking to audiences in the open air, after the Sunday evening service in the chapel, and generally had a congregation of from 3000 to 4000 persons, who listened with the most patient and respectful attention."

He went on to express the wish that working men should be made to feel really welcome in God's house. "Churches and Chapels filled with people of all classes, and wherein distinctions of social rank should be all forgotten, would be far better than Churches and Chapels half filled with the wealthier sort, and halls and theatres crowded with working people."

Again one notes a reference to "half filled" churches—perhaps surprising in view of the belief on which we were brought up that Churches were full in Victoria's reign. But the statement is confirmed by Ramsay Muir in his History of Liverpool.

". . . Liverpool is, at the opening of the twentieth century, not a very religious place. Numerous as the Churches are, they could not possibly contain more than a small proportion of the population, *and many of them are half-empty*. The majority of the inhabitants of Liverpool seem to be outside of the direct influence of the Churches." (my italics.)

But for Hugh Stowell Brown the position was different.

"I for one have no reason to complain of working men keeping aloof from religious ordinances. I think we have pretty nearly, if not quite, a thousand of them in constant and devout attendance upon the means of grace at Myrtle Street Chapel. I do not, however, know how far my lectures on Sunday afternoon may have contributed to this."

Another contributory factor may have been the Workman's Bank which was set up by his Church. "The Institution was formed in 1861 and within twenty three years three thousand people, nearly all of the working class, had deposited £80,000, a figure which would have to be multiplied many times to get the equivalent value today. Writing of the Bank, he said:—

"All that any of us desired was to foster habits of thrift and economy, and with very little idea that the concern would ever become what it is; expecting, or rather hoping, that perhaps two or three hundred of the working people would be encouraged to save something out of their earnings . . . It is a great satisfaction to me to feel that we have so far secured the confidence of a very large number of working people. We have had two runs upon the bank. When Barned's Bank failed one depositor ran upon us and demanded the ten shillings we owed him; and when the Royal Bank broke up we had to stand the rush upon us of another fifteen shillings. This, I understand, is the extent to which our institution has been viewed with diminished confidence during the recent terrible times."

The Workman's Bank continued until its role was taken over by the Post Office Savings Bank.

By the time he entered his fifty fifth year and after over thirty years ministry in the same Church it is perhaps not surprising to find him writing:—

"I felt that after thrty four years of brain work such as mine has been, the mind needs a long repose at least for a full year. I felt that I had pretty well preached myself out; and could no longer do justice to myself, to the Church, or to the Master whom I serve." He reckoned he had preached at Myrtle Street about four thousand sermons.

He tendered his resignation on the 13th August 1880 but received a Memorial signed by over a thousand members of the Church and congregation begging him to continue. He carried on for six more years till his death.

He could hardly have been more successful. To be called to the Ministry so young, to remain the Minister of one Church for over forty years and to see the Church grow and prosper and become the centre of a group of Churches and Missions, to maintain very large congregations and increase Church membership—what more could any Minister wish for? In his own words, written at the time when he was thinking of retiring:—

"The Church was in a most healthy and prosperous condition. It was out of debt; it had considerable funds for charitable purposes; there were no signs of dissension or disaffection towards myself. Looking at it all round, in influence, funds, membership, and schools, the concern was in good order and condition, and I felt it was fit to be handed over to a successor free from everything that might be considered a trouble or disadvantage."

So far so good, but he saw a small cloud on the horizon.

"Gradually the extension of the town, and the prevailing fashion of going to live in the suburbs, had made it increasingly difficult to obtain a large congregation, but I felt justified in believing that for many years to come the place might fairly hold its own as one of the best positions in Liverpool.

"Though it may savour of conceit to say so, I felt well assured that the present congregation consists largely of persons who attend simply because they prefer my ministry to any other they can find, and I could not but suppose that if I perservered in my intention of resigning there might be a moving away, which would largely diminish the attendance, and consequently the revenue. Though I regarded this prospect with much anxiety, I felt also that, in any case, the man who comes after me will have to keep and gather his own people, and if he be the right man for the place he will do so."

When he spoke of the difficulty of obtaining a large congregation he was thinking in thousands. The men who came after him were going to find it difficult to gather hundreds and thought they were doing well if they did so.

Meanwhile there was an even more famous Baptist preacher in London. In Hugh Stowell Brown's Common Place Book there is an entry which reads:—

"One of Spurgeon's Colporteurs writes to me, begging me for the sake of his two Masters, C. H. Spurgeon and the Lord Jesus Christ (such is the order of precedence), to help in his work."

R. C. K. Ensor in his "England 1870–1914" has written of Charles Haddon Spurgeon, "if native eloquence and wide popular appeal be the test"—he "must be ranked among the greatest English preachers of any age." He was born in 1834 and died in 1892. For thirty years he had preached in the Metropolitan Tabernacle which could seat 4600 and frequently contained another thousand. On one occasion eight thousand were counted out of the building. For thirty years the Church was full. Of his printed weekly sermons more than a hundred million copies were sold. On one occasion alone his publishers "received an order for a million copies". Once at the Crystal Palace he preached to 23,654 persons and on several occasions in the open air he preached to congregations of between ten and fifteen thousand. To hear him at the Tabernacle one had to either have a ticket or queue early. Just as in the fifties and sixties of the Twentieth Century men and women crossed the Atlantic to see Olivier act, so in the last century they came to hear Spurgeon preach.

He gave three sermons a week. He prepared his Sunday Morning sermon on Saturday evening and his Sunday evening sermon only on Sunday afternoon. He spent considerably more time on revising his sermons for publication.

Writing after his death in the Morning Advertiser it was said:—

"Charles Spurgeon passed through the greatest peril that can beset a man's character, and he came out of it not only unscathed, but with an ever-increasing reputation. A preacher who attains unbounded popularity at twenty is exposed to temptations which few can successfully withstand. He was for a year or two the sensation of the town. The cleverest satirical writers of the period made him the butt of their almost constant attacks. Exaggerated praise on the one hand, and ignorant and ill-tempered vituperation on the other, would have effectually spoiled any but a man of genuine sincerity. But fame was by no means Mr. Spurgeon's only snare. From an early period in his career he has been trusted with the dispensing of enormous sums of money. Others, also, have been similarly trusted, have doubtless been equally honest, but it has happened to few to escape, as he has done, even the breath of suspicion."

He used money which was given to him amongst other things for the Metropolitan Tabernacle, to the building of which more than a million people contributed. When it opened for worship it was free of debt. In 1869 Spurgeon's

Orphanage was opened—opened to children of all denominations. He also started a college for training ministers which he called Pastors College—but became better known as Spurgeon's College. "This is my life's work, to which I believe God has called me," he said, "and therefore I must do it. To preach the gospel myself, and to train others to do it, is my life's object and aim."

By 1879 the Daily Telegraph was writing:—

"Suddenly a change sprang up, numbers of young men, inspired by the teaching of Mr. Spurgeon, went out into the villages and hamlets, preaching a crusade against indifference. Eyed contemptuously by the dignitaries of the Church, and coldly by the leaders of Dissent, they were yet warmly received by the people to whom they appealed . . .

"Fired by the example of the peripatetic preacher and of the young disciples of Mr. Spurgeon, who, proceeding from his College, have baptised right and left the converts to their views, the old-fashioned Non-conformist Minister has roused himself to greater activity, and bestirred himself to maintain the position that was for the moment imperilled."

The students were encouraged to preach at Churches whilst they were still at college. By the time he died "nearly nine hundred men had been trained for the Ministry". Spurgeon exhorted his students to study Richard Baxter, John Bunyan and George Whitefield and amongst his pieces of advice were the following:—

"Follow the example of the cook, who, when she sends up a well-cooked dinner does not send up the cooking utensils with it. You do the same, leave your cooking utensils in the study, and give the people the result of their use, and see that you prepare something worthy to set before them."

"The best preacher is the man who charges his gun with all he knows, and then, before he fires, puts himself in."

"A large Church is to be preferred to a small one: the latter has many attractions, but it is not unlike a row-boat which a man is in danger of upsetting if he moves about, whereas the former is like an ocean steamer, on which he can parade without the possibility of upsetting the whole concern."

Or more briefly—prepare thoroughly but be or appear to be spontaneous in the pulpit; give it all you've got and more; don't be afraid of thinking big in terms of churches.

His words had a considerable effect on his students, not least posthumously on one who was born in 1887.

Through the night of doubt and sorrow
Onward goes the pilgrim band,
Singing songs of expectation,
Marching to the Promised Land.

Clear before us through the darkness
Gleams and burns the guiding light;
Brother clasps the hand of brother
Stepping fearless through the night.

One the object of our journey,
One the faith which never tires,
One the earnest looking forward,
One the hope our God inspires.

One the gladness of rejoicing
On the far eternal shore,
Where the One Almighty Father
Reigns in love for evermore.

Onward, therefore, pilgrim brothers,
Onward with the Cross our aid;
Bear its shame, and fight its battle,
Till we rest beneath its shade.

Soon shall come the great awaking,
Soon the rending of the tomb;
Then the scattering of all shadows,
And the end of toil and gloom.

S. BARING-GOULD from the Danish

B

Three

Escape from the Welsh Valleys

By the early twenties Liverpool was beginning to recover from the staggering casualties of the First World War. From this dirty, wet city the big Atlantic liners still sailed from the Pier Head, past H.M.S. Conway—an old wooden training ship where John Masefield had been a cadet—past the oval shaped paddle steamer ferries H.M.S. Daffodil and H.M.S. Iris, survivors of the Zeebrugge raid, and over the workings of the new Mersey tunnel. The sky-line was dominated immediately by three buildings, Liver, Cunard and Docks, the melee of docks a tangle of cranes, funnels, masts and rigging and behind rising slowly the red sandstone mass of the Neo Gothic Anglican Cathedral designed by the Roman Catholic Sir Giles Gilbert Scott while the Anglican Lutyens was planning an even more splendid Roman Catholic Cathedral. Not far away Sir Henry Seagrave was establishing a world land speed record on the sands of Southport; the greatest centre forward in the world, Dixie Dean, was heading his marvellous goals for Everton and the fastest bowler in the world, MacDonald, was bowling for Lancashire and standing up to him was the greatest wicket keeper in the world, George Duckworth—or if not the greatest the one with the loudest appeal. Once a year the world's greatest horse race was run—the Grand National.

The chocolate and cream trams rattled and lurched round the Pier Head and through the main shopping centre out through the red brick and blue slated Victorian suburbs to the semi-green world of the post war semi-detached.

In the streets there were people of all races and colours.

Chinese restaurants had not become fashionable but Chinese laundries were common. Drunken men reeling along the side walks were a frequent sight. Magnificent hearses drawn by splendid black horses passed by as men lifted their hats and caps. The bands of the Scouts, the Boys Brigade and the Orange men were out marching almost every Sunday. The finest firework display I have ever seen marked the visit of King George V and Queen Mary.

Here in 1923, to become the minister of the most important Baptist Church in Liverpool, Myrtle Street, arrived a thirty six year old Welsh speaking Welshman. Dark haired, good looking, full of Welsh charm, he was gifted with a beautiful voice and the power to move the hearts of men and women. He was on top of the world and could have reasonable expectations of the world to come. The best was yet to be, as he was so fond of quoting from Browning in his sermons.

Financially for a Baptist Minister he was very well off. His income was £600 a year, he had free use of a manse owned by the Church and he earned perhaps another £100 a year from preaching engagements up and down the country but particularly in Lancashire and North Wales. He could afford to smoke, buy books, good furniture and clothes, have a domestic servant, run a car and educate his son at fee paying schools. Taking into account the change in rates of taxation and the fall in the value of money, he probably enjoyed a standard of living which the £3000 to £4000 a year man today would find it very hard to afford.

By the time he reached Liverpool, he had travelled a long journey from the valleys of South Wales where men were born and bred and lived and died in small communities, enclosed in narrow valleys, working dangerously amid industrial squalor on an apocalyptic scale, finding consolation in the Bible and the Non-Conformist Chapels, where in congregations great and small they lifted their souls on the impassioned fervour of their preacher and the wings of song to soar in the heavens above the hell on earth in which they lived.

"I will call upon the Lord who is worthy to be praised: so shall I be saved from mine enemies.
The sorrows of death compassed me, and the floods of ungodly men made me afraid.
The sorrows of hell compassed me about: the snares of death prevented me.
In my distress I called upon the Lord, and cried unto my God: he heard my voice out of his temple, and my cry came before him, even into his ears.
Then the earth shook and trembled; the foundations also of the hills moved and were shaken, because he was wroth.
There went up a smoke out of his nostrils, and fire out of his mouth devoured: coals were kindled by it.
He bowed the heavens also, and came down: and darkness was under his feet."

"Then the earth shook and trembled; the foundations also of the hills moved . . ."

From The Times 11th–15th December 1880:—
"The explosion at Pen-y-Graig, Glamorganshire, yesterday morning was of a very extensive character and its effects were felt for miles around. A loud explosion occurred at shafts half a mile apart. A publican, living some distance from the old workings, states that his house shook in a most remarkable manner, and he was greatly frightened, not knowing what had happened. He came to the conclusion that an earthquake had occurred. The event happened at 20 minutes past 1 o'clock, when the night shift of 88 men was in the pit . . .

"In a very short time there was an assemblage of about 15,000 persons, all very orderly. The news of the occurrence had been circulated throughout the whole of the Rhonda

Valley, and hundreds of persons flocked up from all the mining villages . . . 84 lives have . . . been lost . . .

"Within easy walk of the village is the Dinas Colliery, the scene of an explosion in 1879; Tynewydd, famous for the brave deeds of the entombed colliers and their rescuers, is but a short distance further on towards Pontypridd; Cymmu Colliery, where hundreds of men were killed by a catastrophe similar to that which has just happened, is close by; while three miles to the westward is Ferndale, the scene of two great colliery explosions . . .

"The very coffins stored by the Dinas Company for the men who were never recovered are now being brought upon men's shoulders to meet the exigencies of the present case . . .

"It was only a few days ago that a meeting of the men's representatives was held at Cardiff to hear an explanation from a Rhymney Baptist minister of a process which had been discovered of rendering the use of naked candles innocuous . . .

"Most of the deceased men leave families, several of them very large families. In some cases men went down the pits to work for the first time last night, never to return alive . . .

"An exceedingly painful scene was witnessed when the explorers came upon the bodies of Edward Lewis, local preacher with the Wesleyans, and his little son 13 years of age. He had a large family, and had taken his little boy to assist him in the pit. He was evidently carrying the boy in his arms when he fell, for the father was found on his face and the boy tightly clasped in his arms. Dr. Henry Naunton-Davies, one of the surgeons, points out the singular fact that nearly all the bodies had the jawbones fractured, and that almost without exception the principal injuries were to the face . . . in one part of the workings the coal dust lying in the roadway had been converted into cinders. In some places brattice-cloth stools stood entire as when placed there, but the moment they were touched they crumbled into ashes . . .

"A list of Welsh colliery accidents during the last 35 years will be read with interest at the present time:—

"August 2, 1845—Cronbach, near Merthyr Tydvil, 28 lives lost; January 14, 1846—Risca Colliery, 35 lives lost; June 21, 1848—Victoria, Monmouth, 11 lives lost; August 11, 1849—Lletty Shenkiu, Aberdare, 52 lives lost; September 3, 1851, Aberdare (chain broke), 14 lives lost; May 10, 1852—Duffryn Pit, Aberdare, 64 lives lost; May 10, 1852—Gwaendraeth Vale (water broke in), 28 lives lost; March 12, 1853—Risca Vale explosion, 10 lives lost; November 29, 1855—Cwmainman, Aberdare (cage upset), 8 lives lost; July 15, 1856—Cymmer, Pontypridd, 114 lives lost; October 13, 1858—Primrose Colliery, Swansea, 13 lives lost; same year—Duffryn, near Newport, 20 lives lost; April 6, 1859—Chain Colliery, near Neath (flooded), 26 lives lost; December 1, 1860—Risca Colliery, Newport, 45 lives lost; February 19, 1862—Gethin Colliery, Merthyr Tydvil, 40 lives lost; October 17, 1863, Morfa, Glamorganshire, 31 lives lost; December 26, 1864—Maesteg, Glamorganshire, 14 lives lost; June 16, 1865—New Bedwellty pit, Tredegar, 26 lives lost; December 25, 1865—Upper Gethin mine, Merthyr Tydvil, 30 lives lost; November 8, 1867—Ferndale Colliery, Rhondda Valley, 178 lives lost; June 10, 1869—Ferndale Colliery, 60 lives lost; July 23, 1870—Llansamlet, near Swansea, 19 lives lost; March 2, 1871—Victoria, Monmouth, 19 lives lost; October 4, 1871—Gladys pit, Aberdare, 4 lives lost; January 10, 1872—Oakwood, Llynvi Valley, Bridgend, 11 lives lost; December 4, 1875—Powell Duffryn, New Tredegar, 22 lives lost; December 5, 1876—Llan Colliery, Pentyrch, 12 lives lost; December 18, 1876—Abertillery, Monmouth, 20 lives lost; September 11, 1878—Prince of Wales Colliery, Abercarn, 269 lives lost; January 13, 1879—Dinas Colliery, 68 lives lost; July 15, 1880—Risca Colliery, 120 lives lost."
From The Times 24th–28th December 1885:—
"An alarming colliery explosion took place today at the Mardy Colliery . . . situated near Ferndale, and has resulted in a supposed loss of 300 lives . . . The work of the mine proceeded in the ordinary way until a quarter to 3 o'clock,

when a terrific report, accompanied by a huge volume of flame belching forth from the downcast shaft (through which 800 men had descended to their work) proclaimed . . . that there had occurred one of those terrible calamities which are the dread of mining communities . . . It being Christmas time, many of the female inhabitants were away from home busy making their purchases in preparation for the season but still there were a large number of women by their firesides waiting for the men, who would return in the ordinary course at 5 o'clock. Among these the alarm was something terrible to contemplate as, hurrying on bonnets and shawls, they rushed down to the mouth of the pit in excited groups . . . There are at present thousands round the mouth of the pit, and the mountains on either side, from the number of lighted lamps seen, show that great numbers are making their way to the scene of the catastrophe from the adjoining valleys . . .

"Accidents are reported to have occurred at two adjoining pits at Merthyr Tydvil. At Abercanaid the breakdown of a pumping engine resulted in the accumulation of water in the pit to the depth of six feet, and 700 men were thus rendered idle, while at the south pit 100 colliers narrowly escaped death, old workings having inadvertently been broken into . . .

"The following are narratives by survivors . . .

'I heard the earth tremble . . . we saw doors blown to pieces . . . at last some 120 tons of the roof fell in . . . we smelt sulphur strongly—we saw many corpses'
(among whom were lads and boys of 17, 16, 14, 13, and 12 years of age).

"The ministers of religion have been flitting to and fro . . . now summoned to some bedside where it was feared death was at hand, and now to some house of mourning to see how the widows and orphans of their flocks were bearing up against their sorrow. The great majority of the miners and their families are Dissenters—Independents, Baptists and Methodists, with little unpretending chapels, bearing such names as Siloam, Zion and Bethany; while there is also a small congregation attached to the Established Church, and worshipping in a tiny hall. Each of these congregations has lost some of its members and adherents, but the Baptists most of all . . .

"Besides the bodies that will be buried here, there are several that will be carried over the high hills to Aberdare, from which many of the younger men came. The bearing of them thither will be an exceedingly difficult task, for the road is but a mountain path impossible to be traversed by any vehicle . . .

"About 40 of the victims of the explosion have either been interred or have been sent away to their old homes for interrment. Fourteen were sent away from Mardy yesterday at half past 5. The scene was most impressive; hundreds of extemporised torches weirdly illuminated the darkness as the bodies were carried from the temporary lodgement to the railroad siding, an old Welsh resurrection hymn being sung the while, and much emotion prevailed . . ."

From The Times 27th–30th August 1892:—

"A colliery explosion of a most disastrous character occurred at 20 minutes past 8 o'clock yesterday morning at Park Ship Colliery, Aberkenfig, near Bridgend, South Wales, resulting in great loss of life . . . A terrific explosion took place. It was heard for miles around . . . The explosion was followed by huge columns of smoke and fire . . . Men, women and children rushed to the entrance of the colliery with horror depicted on their faces . . . the ground shook as if from an earthquake, and houses half a mile away trembled . . ."

From The Times 25th–27th June 1894:—

"One of the most appalling disasters ever known in the South Wales coalfield occurred on Saturday afternoon at the Albion Colliery, Cilfynydd, near Pontypridd, in the Taff Valley . . . During the great coal strike, when troops were imported into South Wales to quell the riots, it was selected as the headquarters of the cavalry . . . at about a quarter to

4 o'clock a loud report was heard, followed almost immediately by another, and the mouth of the pit was immediately enveloped in thick black smoke, through which tongues of flame shot into the air . . . . Up to yesterday afternoon 244 bodies had been recovered from the Albion Colliery and 201 had been identified. The colliery authorities find that the estimated number of the killed is much too low and it is feared that over 300 lives have been lost. In one house lie the bodies of a father, four sons, and six lodgers."
From The Times 25th–31st May 1901:—

"A terrible explosion is reported from the Universal Colliery in the Aber Valley, near Caerphilly . . . there were 83 men below ground . . . and all except one man . . . have inevitably perished . . . the task of the explorers has latterly been seriously hindered by the stench arising from the mine . . . enormous quantities of the roof have been brought down . . . the danger to the explorers is much increased by the prospect of further falls of rock, and much time is consumed in constantly propping up portions of the roof as the work proceeds . . . Of the victims in Friday's explosion . . . the bodies of 51 have been recovered up to last night . . . the work of exploration is now being expeditiously pursued, and only two districts in the western side remained unexplored. It is in this locality, which lies near to the Albion Colliery where in 1894 no fewer than 276 miners perished, that evidence of the explosion is likely to be found . . ."
From The Times 12th–15th July 1905:—

"A terrible colliery explosion, so disastrous that there is reason to fear that for loss of life it will rank with the worst accidents in the South Wales coalfield, occurred at midday yesterday at the extensive colliery at Wattstown in the Rhondda Valley . . .

"One of the most remarkable features of this explosion was the very large number of young men and boys who were killed . . .

"As the day wore on the crowds had increased from
B*

hundreds to thousands; the approaches to the colliery were impassable, and the mountain sides were black with people . . .

"Mr. W. Abraham, M.P., arrived on the scene of the accident about 1 o'clock yesterday . . . (he) said:— 'It is heart-rending, pitiful, discouraging. We had hoped we had arrived at a solution, as to how these accidents could be avoided, but here we have Clydach Vale and Wattstown upsetting all our calculations. We are still in the dark and it is the darkness that is so discouraging . . .'

"The gloom hanging over the Rhondda Valley yesterday when the first batch of funerals . . . took place, was intensified by the thunderclouds which every moment threatened a downpour. Blinds were drawn and shop windows shuttered along the whole route . . .

"Between 12,000 and 15,000 people went to pay their last tribute of respect to their fallen comrades . . . People reached Ynyshir from all parts, by train, in brakes, and on foot across the mountains from the other valleys . . . At half past 2 the first funeral started, and then they came one after another in one huge procession, in each case headed by a coffin borne on a bier, for there were no hearses . . . On arriving at the gates (of the cemetery) the choir sang such hymn tunes as 'Aberystwyth' and 'Ebenezer', and other well-known Welsh hymns . . . From 4 o'clock until 6 a continual stream of coffins and mourners went through the gates . . .

"A terrible accident occurred yesterday afternoon at New Boston pit . . . near St. Helens, resulting in the deaths of the colliery manager and four other men, whilst three miners sustained terrible injuries . . . about 12 yards of the roofing fell upon the unfortunate men . . .

"Three miners lost their lives on Saturday through the flooding of a portion of the workings at the Sheyd Colliery Bloxwich . . .

"An accident involving the loss of two lives occurred on Saturday morning at Bebside Colliery, near Newcastle-on-Tyne. Trials were being made with new ropes and machinery

. . . a wheel pillar became dislodged, and dragged a quantity of the timber which supports the roof . . ."
From The Times 15th–20th October 1913:—
First Leader

"We are but giving voice to the universal feeling of the country and the Empire when we offer hearty congratulations to the young royal pair who this day enter into the Holy Estate of Matrimony. It is long since we had a Royal wedding in London, and this one is of rather unusual interest. Bride and bridegroom are alike British . . ."
Second Leader

"Yesterday morning, at Senghenydd, which lies in the centre of the South Wales coalfield, occurred what may unhappily prove to be the most serious calamity that has overtaken a British coalmine within the memory of man. After a violent explosion the mine appears to have taken fire. It was the time of day when the most numerous shift, nearly a thousand men, were at work. Over four hundred miners are still imprisoned by the flames, and their supply of good air is apparently cut off . . .

"The colliery is surrounded on three sides by mountains, and, bare of trees or shrubs, they are stern and rather gloomy hills that frown down on the valley as it descends to the uniform streets of the colliery town. Within this amphitheatre thousands of people gathered today . . . Men tramped over the hills from the parallel valley or walked up from Caerphilly and the lowlands south of its ancient fortress, to aid, to comfort, and to watch. They were massed on the colliery premises or on the surrounding hillsides from morning until night. I have never seen so silent a throng . . . Few words were spoken by the vast crowd as the hours toiled slowly on. They waited for news, and the only news they got was bad news. Women and children, mothers and wives, sons and daughters of the men underground waited patiently at the pit mouth for tidings of their loved ones. There was little display of emotion . . . and there was a grimness in the demeanour of this anxious but strong-nerved crowd which added terribly to the poignancy of the spectacle. The women particularly seemed to be steeling themselves against the knock-down blows which are the lot of miners' wives . . .

"Many of the older men who escaped the disaster of May 1901, are among the number now missing . . .

"Families of five and seven are among the killed and missing. One woman has lost her husband, three sons, and four brothers . . .

"The main road from the pit bottom runs for about two miles and a half, or about an hour's journey, to the coal face . . .

"A number of dead bodies have been brought up today . . . Many of the poor fellows have the appearance of having been overcome by a kind of frozen sleep . . . Down in the mine they found a father and his son dead in each other's arms . . . many were 'gassed', and bore no marks at all; others met a violent death from the blast . . .

"A member of one of the rescue parties was killed exploring the workings this morning . . .

"The tension, the silence, the gnawing anxiety, are horrible beyond comparison with anything that I and my colleagues have ever witnessed . . . Women are breaking down under the strain, and even the outward show of men is faltering. The crushing burden of the catastrophe is only just beginning to be realised . . . We talk in awed tones of the decimation of a regiment in a bloody battle, but here a great community engaged in the pursuit of a peaceful vocation is threatened with the loss of at least a quarter of its able-bodied manhood. That list of 375 missing may make such a tale of loss and suffering as has never been told before in our industrial history . . ."

In fact the number was not 375. It was 439. A rescuer was asked what it was like below. He replied, "If you have got some idea what hell is like, that is it."

In another South Wales Valley decades later children then

unborn were killed when the tip at Aberavon slid down the hill.

There is a ghastly monotony about these disasters—a terrible explosion, the rush to the pithead, the gathering silent crowds on the hillsides, the bravery of the rescuers, the bodies being brought up, messages of sympathy from the owners often resident outside Wales, the numbers among the dead of lads and boys of 12, 13, 14, 15, 16 and 17 years of age, the drawn blinds, the long funeral processions and the appeal funds launched by the Lord Mayor of London.

These are examples of some of the big disasters. The statistics for the principal colliery disasters caused by explosions of firedamp or coal dust in England and Wales from 1851 to 1922 show that in that period 8571 miners were killed, of whom 3179 were killed in the South Wales and Monmouth district, many more than those killed in any other district. In the period from 1871 to 1900—the period just before and after my father was born—1859 were killed, an average of one death a week.

But these were only the big disasters and only disasters caused by explosions. Behind the cataclysmic big explosions which caused a temporary stir in public sympathy was a daily worse horror. Even while the big disasters were being reported in the extracts given above, other smaller accidents were occurring. The Leader writer of The Times on the 15th October 1913 said:—

"Statistics show that *each day* the mines of the United Kingdom claim rather more than three victims; in some pit or other the miners, following their traditional method of showing respect for their dead, leave their work and return to their homes." An analysis of 11,165 deaths occurring in coal mines during the ten years ending with 1884 showed that while 2,562 were due to explosions, 4,582 were caused by falls of the sides or roofs, and 4,021 were attributable to other causes.

A letter to The Times on the 28th December 1885 in

support of an appeal by the Monmouthshire and South Wales Miners' Permanent Provident Society after the explosion at the Mardy Colliery said:—

"I may be permitted to mention that the Permanent Society, although this is the first occasion on which it has had to deal with an accident causing many deaths, is already maintaining 110 widows and 190 children. This large family has been gathered from the single accidents constantly occurring in our coal-field, of which the public seldom hear, but which in the aggregate cause far more suffering and distress than the large disasters . . ."

Writing in support of the appeal following the 1894 disaster when 290 were killed, the Lord Mayor of London said:—

"The men at this colliery have not been improvident. All the deceased were members of the Monmouthshire and South Wales Miners' Permanent Provident Society, under whose rules, *the widows and children are entitled to 5s. per week and 2s. 6d. respectively.* To provide this very modest allowance I am told that nearly £50,000 will be required, and it must be remembered that these permanent funds are of comparatively recent growth and are imperilled by such a great and exceptional demand upon their resources. In the case of the South Wales fund, for example, there are on the books 60 widows and 1100 children, the vast majority of whom have been rendered dependent by accidents causing one or two deaths, of which the public never hear . . ."

Death in an explosion killing scores and hundreds, death from roof falls and flooding, from suffocation and the traps of machinery; and with the dead there were the others, the lucky survivors, the injured and all the time day by day, the coal dust was being quietly sucked into the lungs, building up a slower more drawn out death agony over the years.

My father missed death or injury when a roof collapsed over where he had been a minute or two earlier.

I was over thirty years old before I went down a coal

mine for the first and only time. It was a modern colliery working with machinery, cutters and conveyors. In the main roadway the steel hooped support girders were buckling. You could not stand up to work at the face. It was hot, coal dust wreathed the air, and there was darkness at noon. The sputum and blood on our coal is washed off before it is delivered to our cosy homes with their cosy open-hearth fires. Please don't tell me that the phrase "blood on our coal" is a cliché.

To get to Liverpool my father had taken one of the classic escape routes. A brother became a Congregational Minister; one of his sisters emigrated to America. Two sisters stayed in Wales. The first husband of one was killed in the 1914–18 war. The husband of the other became unemployed in the thirties and was supported by his wife's work making trousers at home for a pittance.

Having left school at 13 years of age, my father managed to get accepted as a young man at Spurgeon's College. He was offered his first church while still a student and left before taking his degree to become in 1913 the Minister of a Baptist Church at Leyton in London. During the 1914–18 war he went to France with the Y.M.C.A. until he was invalided home with trench fever. He found his church emptied by the bombing raids of Zeppelins. He married an English girl and in 1919 moved to a church at Muswell Hill. Although he often returned to preach in Welsh and English, for holidays and to visit his family, he never went back to live in Wales.

He was not the kind of preacher of whose sermon it was said that it was read, badly read and not worth reading. Nor did he practise the method of:— "First I tell 'em what I'm going to tell 'em; then I tell 'em; then I tell 'em what I've told 'em." He devoted a great deal of trouble and energy to his sermons in and out of the pulpit. He read widely and kept up to date in theology and science, he maintained a library of several thousand books, he spent hours on each sermon, he made notes, for years he preached each sermon first to his long suffering wife and then when he got into the pulpit he hardly ever looked at his notes. He spoke with humour, and intensity, there were quiet passages and crescendo passages, there was fire and passion, there was agony and sweat. In hot weather he often changed completely after the morning service and after the evening service he sank back exhausted in the calm and quiet of a job well done. He had the Welsh hwyl—an untranslatable word but which has been described by D. Parry Jones:

"The old preachers filled the church with invisible kings, gods, devils, saints and angels; they impersonated spiritual heroes; they sang, they shouted, they warned, they pleaded, eventually soaring into a peroration—the hwyl—entirely now at the mercy of the spirit that had gradually worked them up to this final and sustained climax.

"As they now sang their words, in an emotional rapture and disciplined abandon, the congregation swayed with them. Then suddenly, always suddenly, came the end where they dive-bombed us with their final sentences and with a devastating affect. After this sudden crash came the calm, and men and women, released from the bonds of oratory, moved in their seats again, turning to their neighbours in glowing appreciation if not in amazement to see them still there after the explosive crash.

"The storm, the drama, was over, the curtain was dropped, the congregation returned to their own bodies and pews, having been transported in fiery chariots of oratory away to Bethlehem, to Jerusalem, to Gethsemane, to Calvary."

Where did my father's style derive from and what was the background in which he was born? While Spurgeon was winning fame in London the Welsh Revival movement was working itself out in Wales.

Calvinistic Methodism had led the Revival towards the end of the Eighteenth Century and had spread to the Independents and Baptists. Thomas Charles of Bala had left the

Established Church and under him the Methodists became a separate church. He also was one of the founders of the British and Foreign Bible Society which helped to provide Bibles in Welsh homes. By the early Nineteenth Century there were many famous preachers like Christmas Evans, John Elias and Williams of Wern. So great were the crowds they attracted that thousands assembled in the open air to sing hymns and hear a feast of sermons lasting hours over a period of days. By 1880 80% of the population of Wales was Nonconformist. What was the Revival really like? Here is how it appeared to a famous Welshman:—

"I remember being myself in that garden on a Sunday evening, and passing through a 'religious experience' there which I can never forget. It was in the year 1859 or, possibly, 1860. I was about seven years old at the time, and the religious Revival was on in all its power in all the neighbouring dissenting chapels (for some reason or another the Church of England was not liable to these onsets). The evidence of the presence and power of the 'Spirit' was overwhelming then and women were, quite genuinely, beside themselves with religious excitement. They broke out in the services, glorifying God by the help of hymns and verses and not infrequently in language of their own which, owing to their 'exalted' condition, was sometimes marvellous in its power and beauty . . . Often, during these months, did I crouch in the bottom of the pew in order to escape the waving arms of my grandmother—noted for the depth and devotion of her religious life. And I occasionally watched strange scenes amidst the excitement. For instance, I saw a farm labourer—a very shoddy character in fact—on his knees in the big pew, beat in the panels of the pulpit with his bare fists; and I watched the finest of the church elders, one of the ablest men I have ever met, go from end to end of the chapel, and up and down its aisles, on his knees praising God all the time and manifestly in the power of an overwhelming force.

"I am not going to discuss either the causes or the spiritual value of these religious revivals, and I shall say only one thing, namely, that to doubt the sincerity of some, yea, of most of the revivalists, or the permanence of their good effects upon their lives, were dishonest and absurd on my part . . .

"The Revival had come to the neighbouring chapels; or, in other words, to put it quite frankly as we all thought of it, 'The Holy Spirit', the third person in the Trinity had actually arrived at these chapels and attended the meetings. But He had not come into *our* chapel; and great was the searching of hearts. The prayers of the elders became more and more urgent, and the fear grew even more grave that possibly some dark sin on someone's part in our church kept the Holy Spirit away. We were bidden examine and humble ourselves anew, and we did so. But at last the spirit came. It was on the evening on which I was in the garden, under the chapel window. For, did I not hear, and recognise the voices of the women, who were in an ecstatic state, mingling with the voice of the preacher, and for a while, contending with it in wild confusion? I have said that, at the time I was about seven years old, but that did not protect my little child-soul from being suddenly overwhelmed by the conviction that I was not *one of the elect*! My reason for this conclusion was that when the Holy Spirit *did* come I was not in chapel. Manifestly my Calvinistic upbringing was thorough; and even then the main joists of my creed were being laid, and by other hands than my own."

So wrote Sir Henry Jones who succeeded Caird as Professor of Moral Philosophy in the University of Glasgow. He was the son of a shoe maker and died in 1922 and according to the Introduction to his book "Old Memories" from which the above extract is taken, he wrote his memories "during the last two years of his life as a relaxation from the more arduous task of preparing the Gifford lectures, since published under the title *A Faith that Enquires*. Throughout this period he was suffering from cancer, and he well knew that it was surely defeating the doctors and that the end could not long be delayed. He fought against these odds with extraordinary courage, and no one who reads the pages which follow or the radiant exposition of his religious faith in the Gifford Lectures would ever surmise that their author was the victim of a malignant disease and rarely free from pain."

From a very humble, poor and religious background he escaped from Wales through education and the Church to end as an exile in a strange land, dying of cancer—that was the life of Sir Henry Jones—no wonder my father read and re-read his little book.

There have been many Welsh Revival movements but the one to which Sir Henry Jones was referring was the aftermath of the Revival to which Christmas Evans was one of the great inspirations. At page 135 of the biography of Christmas Evans by E. Ebrard Rees it is stated that Evans was invited to preach in English at Lime Street Chapel, Liverpool—the passage is underlined by my father and noted "afterwards Myrtle Street".

The biographer of Chrstmas Evans writes:—

"Christmas Evans was in at the Golden Age of preaching. More than anyone else, he was responsible for that age continuing as long as it did. Others helped to put preaching on the map, but he helped to put the sermon into the soul and blood of Welsh Christians, especially Baptists. The service was of little use to him except as a setting in which the sermon was the precious pearl. The setting was minimised, almost neglected, so that the pearl might flash its brilliance and captivate the congregation by that brilliance . . . When the sermon becomes the everything in a service, much rests on the preacher. He has to bear the responsibility that a hymn or anthem, response or chant or prayer could do were they given proper place and dignity. Small preachers who weed out everything else from the service but their puerile sermons empty more churches than all the other factors. Any preacher who dares to make the sermon all that matters in a service, must be a great preacher with a great message that he can deliver with passion and conviction."

Christmas Evans died in Swansea in 1838. Nearby in the planned village of Moriston my father was born in 1887, born into one of those close knit communities of South Wales which were predominantly Non-Conformist. By 1851 76% of the places of worship in the Swansea area were Non-Conformist according to "Social Change in South West Wales" by Brennan, Cooney and Pollins and the same writers go on to say:—

"Clearly, industrial development in Western South Wales was accompanied by the growth of communities the religious needs of which were provided largely by the Non-Conformist denominations . . . Nonconformity was not only 'the chief agent in the preservation of the Welsh language' which 'led to general and greater literary activity', and the stimulation of 'a demand for education' but also provided a radical element in Welsh life which in political forms meant Liberalism. The democratic machinery of Non-Conformity too, it is said (particularly of the Sunday Schools attended by adults), provided useful experience of administration and initiated working-class people into the mysteries of local government."

My father was born into a Welsh speaking family and Community. It has been estimated that in 1889 in the districts of Llanelli, Amman Valley, Pontardulais, Morriston and Ystalyfera about nine-tenths of the tin-plate workers were monoglot Welshmen and my father's father worked in a tin-plate works. The family were Baptists. And who and what are the Baptists? The beliefs of most Baptists are summarised in the following Declaration of Principle which is contained in the Constitution of the Baptist Union of Great Britain and Ireland:—

"The basis of this Union is:—

"1. That our Lord and Saviour Jesus Christ, God Manifest in the flesh, is the sole and absolute authority in all matters pertaining to faith and practice, as revealed in the Holy

Scriptures, and that each Church has liberty, under the guidance of the Holy Spirit, to interpret and administer His Laws.

"2. That Christian Baptism is the immersion in water into the Name of the Father, the Son, and the Holy Ghost, of those who have professed repentance towards God and faith in our Lord Jesus Christ who 'died for our sins according to the Scriptures; was buried, and rose again on the third day.'

"3. That it is the duty of every disciple to bear personal witness to the Gospel of Jesus Christ, and to take part in the evangelisation of the world."

"Each Church has liberty, under the guidance of the Holy Spirit, to interpret and administer His Laws . . ."

Their history is given in outline in the current annual Baptist Handbook as follows:—

Organised Baptist life in England had two distinct beginnings. In 1611 Thomas Helwys led back from Amsterdam a little group who a few years earlier had sought religious freedom in Holland and who had there formed themselves into a Separatist Church—under the leadership of John Smyth—practising believers' baptism. Helwys was the author of *The Mistery of Iniquity,* the first English printed book to plead for full religious freedom. The successors of Helwys and his friends became known as *General Baptists.* They were Arminian in theology but their church order was not unlike the Presbyterians. In 1633 a group connected with a Calvinistic Separatist church in London broke away on adopting believers' baptism. This was the origin of the so-called *Particular Baptists.* They remained Calvinistic in theology but their church order was of the more "independent" type. The first Baptist Church in Wales was founded in 1649 at Ilston Gower, Swansea. Baptists had founded work in Ireland by the mid-seventeenth century and in Scotland by the mid-eighteenth century. A "New Connexion" of the more evangelical General Baptists was formed in 1770 under the influence of the Methodist revival. During the nineteenth century, through the leadership of John Clifford (1836–1923), this section of General Baptists gradually came closer to the Particular Baptists, who as a result of the work of Andrew Fuller (1754–1815) had been delivered from the self-centredness of hyper-Calvinism. In 1792 William Carey (1761–1834) was instrumental in the formation of the Baptist Missionary Society, which gave new impetus to missionary endeavour. In 1812–13 the Baptist Union of Great Britain and Ireland was formed amongst Particular Churches, and this gradually drew into its fellowship the General Baptists of the New Connexion. Certain Churches that have remained more strictly Calvinist and that in general have refused to have, even at the Lord's Table, any but those who have been immersed, are known as *Strict Baptists*. They have considerable strength in certain parts of England and have three regional Associations and a union of their own: The Strict Baptist Assembly. The Baptist Denomination has, over the years, spread to many lands and is today one of the largest Protestant communions in the world.

So much for their beliefs and their history—but how do they work?

Writing in "Social Change in South West Wales" the authors say:—

"In the Baptist and Congregationalist Churches, which hold that each congregation is a church in itself not requiring any special class or hierarchy of priests but depending on a 'priesthood of true believers', the ordinary member has considerable powers in the running of his church.

"For convenience, each church usually has a salaried minister and also a management committee of deacons. The minister and the deacons are the religious leaders of the Fellowship, and are required to give consideration to all the church's work and to carry out its decisions. They are elected by the general membership of the church. The deacons usually hold office for three or four years but are eligible for re-election. A meeting known as the "Church Meeting" is held usually once a month. It is the representative gathering of the church for worship and fellowship, for the admission and dismission of members, for the reception of reports of Church and Denominational organisations and for discussion and decision.'

". . . Baptist and Congregational Churches are essentially self-governing bodies the leaders of which, the ministers and deacons, cannot act without the consent and approval of members. The ordinary member of such a church evidently has the widest powers over its conduct and policy consistent with reasonably efficient administration and leadership."

Let us put a little flesh and blood on the dry bones of that arid anatomical discussion. The minister of a Baptist Church with a few exceptions has to be chosen by his congregation to become its minister; his salary is dependent on the voluntary offerings of his congregation and if his congregation withers and falls away from dislike or apathy the offerings will not support his income and the minister will have to go. He does not, as does his Anglican counterpart, have an impregnable freehold and a salary independent to some extent from the voluntary contributions of his congregation. The Baptist minister, however much it may be wrapped up, is ultimately a paid performer and if he displeases his audience the theatre will empty.

Writing of Christmas Evans his biographer says:—

"Although he preached like an angel and persuaded many to give up their worldly life, and his winsome words brought peace to souls, he was an utter failure when he came to personal relations with his converts or when he presided at their gatherings. In the pulpit he was a genius and a master. Outside the pulpit he had no winning ways. He was clumsy and awkward. He was touchy and irritated at the least contradiction. He had no tact in dealing with men and women. He would pout and sulk; he would offend people; he would quibble about the least things . . . He had not fully realised that the churches over which he had charge were Baptist churches and that their order was congregational in government. Baptist churches can be led but never driven. Those who have led them have been the greatest successes, and those who drove failures . . . When every member claimed the personal and private right of interpretation of the scriptures, and the priesthood of all believers with its numerous anti-priestly implications; when every church, whether large or small, insisted that it was a complete entity and had an absolute and unqualifiable right to come to certain decisions without regard to or consultation with other churches; when churches refused to co-operate in a common task towards the goal he had in view; he stood on his dignity and an authority he assumed he possessed, and claimed to have a right to govern, dictate, rule as well as lead and show the way. He claimed and demanded authority the churches were not prepared to give him. He was a Baptist Pope or Bishop and never realised that such was a contradiction in terms. Democracy not dictatorship, fits in with Baptist ideals. He was a dictator and did not discover, until it was too late, that dictatorship was a foreign element in the democratic churches that were then coming into being. These could be inspired but not commanded."

How far the above applies to my father I do not know. I was not present at deacons meetings. He was certainly not lacking in winning ways—quite the contrary—but he clearly preferred his preaching to his pastoral role. If a member of his congregation was ill or dying he visited conscientiously but he did not relish visits for social chit chat to those who were well and he could be "touchy and irritated at the least contradiction."

Hugh Stowell Brown in a sermon once said:—

"I am aware that I may scarcely be able to look at this question in a purely impartial manner; but I think that, if I occupied a pew and not a pulpit, I should very much prefer that balance of power, or something approaching it, which a paid ministry secures in a church."

He said that if ministers had the means of living independently of all help from the church, "the churches would soon find that they had not ministers, but masters who would rule them with a rod of iron."

But in his Commonplace Book he wrote:—

"If I had a nice moderate income from independent sources, nothing would please me more, and really I think be better for me, than to become more and more a teacher of the working-classes in Liverpool. Better this than to be simply the servant of a capricious congregation. I do long for a broader life than the Baptist or any other ministry affords. God send it, and that soon!"

However, at first all went well for my father at Liverpool. Although he drew his power of preaching from a Welsh background and put himself, in Spurgeon's words, in the barrel of the gun before firing it, I would be giving a totally misleading impression of his preaching if I conveyed the idea that he was a ranting, raving revivalist appealing to the basic emotions of his congregation by a series of Welsh black magical incantations and abracadabra. The following is an address which he gave in 1929—one of the few which have survived because he knew that it was going to be published. It was given to an assembly of Lancashire and Cheshire Baptist Churches.

"There are doubtless many present who are better fitted to undertake the task which confronts each successive generation —of re-interpreting those lofty ideals which are enshrined in the idea of the Church. We are the children of an age which may well plume itself upon its prodigious gains. Its outstanding feature is one of unparalleled achievement, whilst the year's still in the Spring. These exhilarating victories are the fruit of that inquiring spirit which was born with the Reformation. In a reference to the death of Giordano Bruno, Professor Whitehead remarks: 'His death in the year 1600 ushered in the first century of modern science in the strict sense of the term . . . since a babe was born in a manger, it may be doubted whether so great a thing has happened with so little stir.'

"The disintegration of external authority, despite the temporary shelter it found in false literalism, liberated the human spirit which, impelled by the deep necessities of its own expanding mind, could do none other than search out the fascinating secrets of the new universe. When man's spirit was liberated, his mind was captivated. A casual glance at the results fills one with pride, whilst the majesty of the mind, which tore them from their hiding place, humbles one with awe. Man's mastery over nature is entering upon its final stage, one by one, despite nature's reluctance, her cherished secrets are being wrested from her. He has scaled the heavens and plumbed the seas; the airship and the submarine are as uneventful as the Austin Seven. He is able to control them in their course without human agency, and even make them serve his ends. He has annihilated space, and has triumphed over diseases which once made havoc of life; the very span of life is being rapidly extended. The winds, the tides, the lightning still defy his assaults but, like Ajax of old, he faces them undismayed in the sure confidence that they will yet acknowledge his ascendency. The scientist already predicts with confidence that the new Pandora's box, the atom, will soon disclose its secrets, thus placing at man's service its incalculable stores of energy. The student may not know precisely how this will be accomplished, but there is a unanimous agreement that it is a mere matter of time and patience. The consequences are altogether indescribable. A tumbler of water contains sufficient energy to drive a liner across the Atlantic, whilst a few tons would remove Wales bodily into the middle of the Atlantic—her language would then surely become the speech of the immortals since there would be no place for it on earth. Garrisoned with this inconceivable power, man could determine the geography and the climate of the world at his own will. Artificial heating could transform the Arctic regions into a pleasant summer resort, whilst the Sahara might become a second Mediterranean. This is not mere fanciful dreaming, some of these things are already within the reach of engineering skill—the insuperable obstacle, hitherto, is that the cost of the necessary power would swallow up the world's wealth. Armed with cheap power it becomes an immediate economic proposition. Some thinkers hold that the solution will be reached through harnessing the tides; others believe that it will be derived directly from the sun. Marconi has a vision of mechanical engines deriving their motive force by tuning in to one of the great beam wireless stations which will be established throughout the world, with only the solar rays to feed them. The implications are nothing less than revolutionary; all drudgery will be abolished, the whirring of the wheels of industry will be silenced at last.

"The same sense of wild surmise is ours when we reflect upon the achievements of medical science. The extraordinary results of radio-activity have made possible the conquest of diseases which hitherto have been incurable, even by surgical operation. I was privileged, recently, to attend an extraordinary session of the British Medical Association in Liverpool, when Dr. R. C. Canty, of London, lectured on the results of his own research work on the growth of living tissue cells. It was, in brief, the story of the possible conquest of cancer by radium. We were shown on a cinematograph screen the birth of the cancer germs and the incredible speed with which they spread their havoc through a living organism. It was terrifying in its sheer relentlessness. The lecturer then showed that radium not only arrested the disease but that under its searching light the cells themselves entirely disintegrated. Even more fascinating is that chapter in modern medicine which concerns deficiency diseases. Not only have such dread diseases as scurvy and rickets been practically abolished, but discoveries are daily made which raise the standard of life. A 'C 3' population is doomed. All talk vitamins—the most eloquent are those who know best. What is less widely known is that foods lacking in some of these vitamins can, by being exposed to irradiation by ultraviolet rays, acquire the valuable properties they lack. The minister who finds butter beyond his means will be nourished, if not comforted, by irradiated margarine. Not only so, the food value of most vegetation consists of cellulose. Animals enjoy one advantage, they can digest and extract nourishment directly from this cellulose. They are living laboratories which transform cellulose into nourishing food. The chemist, however, believes the day is not remote when man will imitate the activities of the animal by transforming cellulose in his own laboratory into synthetic food. Professor Baly, of Liverpool, has already succeeded in making synthetic sugar by the action of ultraviolet rays on the colouring matter of plants. Man will be able to imitate the flavours of foods and probably to invent new ones, although this may well seem incredible to those members of this Assembly who have been privileged to lunch at Milton Buildings, Manchester. What a strange new world. Industry has been abolished and now agriculture follows. It will not be a world without serious problems, but it will be a world wherein man has the opportunity to develop his deeper self. As Professor Soddy, that brilliant student, remarks, 'Science is on the verge of discoveries of such momentous importance that coal, gas and electricity will become toys for the children in the nurseries; the entire burden of the struggle for existence will be removed and men afforded the opportunity of cultivating their mental and moral life.' It is evident we stand on the threshold of a new era. All these stupendous gains are within our reach, but there is a price to pay. They are ours if man's resources are not wantonly squandered. The scientist can unlock the door to this alluring world if his labours are uninterrupted by the drums of war. Let us then see to it that men are not deprived of their birthright.

"The by-products of this stupendous movement are already

self-evident. Every sphere of life has felt the reaction. Humanity is on the march. Epstein's statue of Christ disturbs those who cherish a conventional idea of the Good Shepherd, whilst the 'imagist' poetry challenges every rhythmic prejudice. Wherever we turn we see man in the throes of change. A new mentality has been born, so that the old stimuli either provokes a different response, or they have become meaningless. That is a fact of the utmost importance—the trappings of life are so altered that our message evolves no answering thrill in the soul. That is the world whose ministers we are. The Church may win the tolerance men gradually yield to those time-honoured institutions which once enriched the genius of the race, but its message seems as a tale that is told. The thing we are up against is not indifference, still less is it sin—it is a passion for reality, the fruit of that new mentality which science has fostered.

"It is significant that this vibrant life is saturated with idealism. Never did social conditions excite a deeper compassion. Our fathers were moved by the pathos of individual wrongs. It is the peculiar merit of this age that its conscience has been stirred by the entire sorry scheme of things. That is at once our glory and despair, for despite ourselves, our achievements threaten to destroy us. We are idealists without the capacity to express them in living deeds. We have outgrown our power to control life. 'In history,' remarks a thinker, 'every step in advance has also been a step backwards.' Progress is not inevitable—it is morally determined. If you improve machinery at the cost of character, if the slavery of the cotton fields but yields to economic servitude; if our control of nature but makes evident our loss of moral control, is it strange that many should be convinced that the night is irrevocably closing upon us? Everywhere a deep wistfulness betrays itself; an intrusive despair which pathetically seeks self forgetfulness in temporal interests. Like a summer's morning which has lost its radiance, our life is overcast with gloom. The intricacy of this new world but deepens the gloom. Mankind is one in the bundle of life. A famine in India threatens England with the scourge of influenza; war in an obscure village undermines the security of the entire world. The frontiers are down. Is it then surprising that amid the tumult of our stupendous activities there should be the hush of a great expectation? Our gains have been won by sacrifices which make evident the sheer sublimity of man. Like the priest before his altar, the scientist is clothed in the unsullied clothes of disinterestedness. Yet we are in despair. We see in the distance the land of our dreams, but fear we shall never possess it. These are the notes our human orchestra sounds out; a mastery over nature with a propect of inconceivable benefits in the near future, a mentality which we dare not ignore; an idealism which is pregnant with the possibilities of a new Eden on earth and a wistfulness which is born of a sense of impetus. Man is not big enough for the world he has evolved; he yearns for the sublimities, but like a bird whose wings are clipped, he is impotent to respond to the lure of the heights.

Surely, it is tragic that amid this welter of emotion and activity the Church is not functioning. One of her functions is the safeguarding of those values which are only too easily squandered. It is the acceleration of life that explains the situation. However, the facts are obvious. Here and there you can put your fingers on a vigorous community—which unhappily proves nothing. In every case its prosperity may be attributed either to a powerful personality whose exuberant nature would always attract a following, or to a tradition so well organised that it has not yet succumbed. In every city there are Churches whose success is due to the fact that they have become sheltering homes for the morally timid and the intellectually stagnant. The future is not with them—they are doomed to drift in the backwaters of life. Preaching is no solution. An outstanding Liverpool preacher assured me at the beginning of his ministry that his congregation was in Lime Street—it is still there. My friend has done what others of us had achieved already—he has attracted casual members from other congregations. A redistribution of our forces is not a solution of the problem. There is something amiss; we are out of touch with the world.

"The facts are as commonplace as they are pathetic. The industrial classes no longer find expression for their idealism within our walls. The great masses are unmoved and seem totally unconscious of any loss. Within a mile of my own Church there are no less than a hundred thousand people who are de-churched, yet we speak glibly of down-town Churches, as though a label solves the problem. Are there no souls down town? Has suburbia, with its insipid vulgarity, become the art of the external? If we spent a tenth of the money we now squander on the suburbs in a vital ministry of compassion down-town, we might not be shamed by a record of ineffectiveness. Man these places, equip them, inspire them with a new compassion and you will remove the reproach from the Church. The well-to-do can dispense with religion, the poor need it. It is ever good news to them.

"We have also lost—if we ever had them—the intelligentsia. Much of their indifference is a mere pose, but we are not gripping them. In a recent questionnaire on religious belief it was significant that faith was weakest where education and leisure for thought were most prevalent.

"No less striking is the loss of woman. She owes everything to the Church, but has now forsaken her foster-mother. Our membership is steadily diminishing. I know that this is partly the result of pruning, but why is it necessary to use the knife so relentlessly? No, the Church is at the crisis. Any vital consideration of the problems must recognise these facts.

"Let us consider the causes of the impotence of the Church. I ask you to think only of the ultimate causes, since these alone are decisive. There are immediate reasons—our absorption in temporal interests, our passion for physical and mental culture, the tyranny of amusements, though it is not improbable that these things have contributed to the sobriety and general well being of the people. What, however, may be seriously questioned is whether they are the causes of our decay. Are they not largely the result? Are they not an expression of the soul's unrest? We must face the problem in a big way—skirmishing never yet won a war. If men turn from us can we rest until we know the real causes?

"It is simply foolish to say that our standards are too lofty. The heroic note was never sounded out in vain. Courage is the livery of noble hearts. Take a cynical view of man and this question drops. Believe in him, as Jesus did, and the question wakes you with trembling of a night. Above all, let us face it with hope, for ways that seem to lead to the abyss are avenues leading to God. Take large views and remember that the problem ultimately rests on the heart of another.

"What then are the ultimate causes? I suggest three for your consideration.

"1. Science has undermined our view of the universe so that the earth has lost its proud centrality. How beautifully simple faith was. God's creative activity reached its culmination in Eden when the sons of the morning shouted for joy. It was not difficult to believe that of all created things, man was sovereign. The Eternal Artist fashioned His canvas and crowded it with seething life ere He rested in quiet satisfaction. The day inevitably came when this assurance began to waver. The magnitude of the universe baffled the imagination and silenced the joy of man's adoration. Generations since one daring worshipper asked 'What is man that Thou are mindful of him?' But the challenging question was forgotten until our own age when, within an incredibly short time our entire perspective changed. The world became a speck in a system whose immensity overwhelms the heart and man but a gnat whose futile cryings are of no interest to Him Who holds the world as a drop in a bucket. How can we believe? Indeed, is not the entire idea of God a projection of a human desire? Mr. Julian Huxley is convinced that the idea of God is a mere synthesis of what is best in man. Surely we need to recover a right sense of magnitude. Size is a mere nothing. An atom reveals the same symmetry—the same worlds upon worlds—as the universe. We shall attain a larger faith, but meanwhile, our spiritual values are at a discount. The pity is that other cherished things are blotted out also; the standard of right and wrong, the necessity of sacrifice and the hope of the hereafter. It is this uncertainty, which hangs like a weight of lead upon the heart, that explains our modern indifference. Some hold aloof from the Church for the love of sin, but most shrink from us because they have lost that faith in whose strength they once lived. The universe is unfriendly to the yearnings of the soul.

"2. Criticism has undermined our view of the Bible, so that we have lost its constraining authority.

"Of course, it is not truly so—none could rob the book of its authority. The Bible is a garden, which is one reason why its great lovers are all gardeners, like Carey. The critic is only a labourer in the garden, pruning the rose tree here, trenching the genial soil there, gleaning the fruit for the Master. He cannot despoil the garden. What, if, in a shady nook, as they walk in the tingle of some great morning, one wanderer should see one angel whilst his companion sees two? There may have been a hundred for all I know. I should expect the entire angelic host to guard the place where my Lord lay a-resting. What if, in the garden lake, you are uncertain of the nomenclature of the fish. If there be a boat there, may you not lose yourself in voyagings of infinite delight? We need a keener vision. Do what you will with the soil, arrange the garden as you may, so long as I am able to enjoy the flowers I am content; I know my Lover is there and it is 'the veriest school of peace.' Men don't go to a garden for geology, botany or history—they *go* there to steep their souls in gladness. There are those who never thrill to the beauty of flowers—they are so busy defending the garden they miss its fragrant ministry. The pity of it!

C

"That is the real message of the Reformation, so 'England became a nest of singing birds'. Our fathers never insisted that all parts of the garden were of equal value; they knew too well there was straw as well as flowers there. They said, 'We must know the mind of Him Who designed the garden, that mind alone will disclose its loveliness.' There is a Bible within the Bible whose authority alone is infallible. 'A house,' says an old writer, 'though otherwise beautiful, yet if it hath no garden belonging to it is more like a prison than a house.' It is so with life. Spend your time amid the beauty of the garden; let its radiance woo you to a new sweetness, and its unsullied peace saturate you, and so wonderful will its influence be that others will be constrained to visit it, and upon those who have never crossed the threshold the spell of the garden will lay its healing touch. No, you cannot shatter the authority of the Bible, for it is the authority of those eternal things by which men truly live. I know of no task of such delight than that which is laid upon us—of making vivid to our fellows the real authority of the Book of Books.

"3. Behaviourism has undermined our view of morality so that we have lost the constraint of freedom. Indeed, freedom has become a worthless word. Man, we are told, is bound from the womb to the inevitable. This is the most serious problem which confronts the Church today. We gladly recognise the services of this school of thought, but he is indeed blind who fails to see that the entire foundation of conduct is assailed. There is a moral determinism. It is the by-product of the decisions we register—for weal or woe we reap what we sow. We must not confuse this with that teaching which mocks at every possibility of freedom. The one is essentially optimistic, the other is dark with despair. It is the task of the Christian thinkers to vindicate that ethic which not only satisfies the deep instincts of the soul for the eternal, but ennobles the soul by its insistence that man has been dowered with the capacity of choice. The entire drift of a section of modern thought is to deny that emphasis. Dr. Lashley, of

Chicago, trained certain mice to walk along a path of light, but after a slight surgical operation, they lost this capacity to choose the light and would only walk in the dark. So, the surgeon concludes to his own satisfaction that conduct is the by-product of certain physical changes in the brain, and that man is but a mass of chemical reactions.

"That is the challenge which confronts us. The entire spiritual foundation of religion is assailed. Until we frankly face these facts we shall remain ineffective. Whilst we trifle with our airy nullities on the shore's of life's restless sea, the tides of modern doubt and unrest threaten to destroy us. May I be quite frank? A good deal of talk about denominationalism leaves me cold. It is, I know generated by a lofty idealism, but the idealism is uninspired by vision. I want to save my Church, but I am more anxious to save the world. I want to make Baptists, but I am lost unless I can make Christians. If Jesus were here He would do something radical. The measure of my failure to follow Him is in precise degree to my lack of courage. We need an intellectual adventure within the Church to match the unceasing activities without. Most of us are afraid to think. We have become mere sentimentalists—at the mercy of every passing fad. We need a new revival of thought. At the back of the Reformation move Copernicus and Erasmus, a new astronomy and a new learning. It must be so again. I am a little impatient of revivals which leave us in a worse state than we were, which do not touch the real issues. Let us venture into the deeps— our Lord is there and the necessities of the soul which abide for ever.

"Let me remind you of the necessity for the Church. If we believe that Jesus has the spiritual value of God, that in Him, despite the limitations imposed by time and space, that eternal glory which is glimpsed in the loveliness of the earth and the poetry of all moving things, that in Him it flowered into fulness of life; that the Incarnation, which was consummated on the Cross, gathers up in one shining life all the scattered hints of God—then there is an eternal necessity for the Church. She is not a mere concomitant of history, but an embodiment of unseen realities. The Church is the effulgence of God. Embracing all our differences, independent of racial, cultural or social conditions—like a plant in a dark cellar she makes for the sun, for she is herself the child of the light. She was born, not in time, she comes radiantly from the heart of God yet her earthly texture is woven of the love that knits the soul to God. He is her Maker, so she will endure despite the frailty of her adherents, their wilful perversions, and their creeds which mar His beauty. The Church is ecstasy, heroism, holiness, love; she is the home of the divinest things. Her very trappings are touched with that mystery which evokes our instinctive reverence. No less an ideal can satisfy our passionate yearnings; when I am united with her I am liberated from the tyranny of base desires, and enter the fellowship of those heroic souls whose sufferings redeem the world. Do you wonder there is a song in my heart? A secret gladness which reveals itself in the fragrance of my life? The Church is the soul's trysting place: within her alluring spaces my Lover walks. Her membership is but for those who have been gifted with the power to know Him, who could not endure life's challenge without the assurance of something stable, perpetual in time, but not of it, nor knowing the blight of its decay.

"Not only so, the Church is no less grounded in a human necessity. The problem is an intensely practical one, it refuses to be dismissed. Everyone is dreaming of a better world, Utopias find a lodging place in every heart. There is the League of Nations with its daring vision of a warless world. But does anyone seriously believe that it can realise that vision? There must be some radical transformation. The League was founded for the express purpose of maintaining those boundaries which were fixed by the victorious powers. These powers still dominate its activities. Take Articles X and XVI. 'The members of the League undertake to respect and preserve as against external aggression the territorial integrity and existing political independence of all the members of the League. In case of any such aggression, or in case of any threat or danger of such aggression, the Council shall advise upon the means by which this obligation shall be fulfilled'. 'Should any member of the League resort to war in disregard of its covenants under Articles XII, XIII, and XIV it shall, ipso facto, be deemed to have committed an act of war against all the members of the League, which hereby undertake immediately to submit it to the severance of all trade or financial relations, the prohibition of all intercourse between their nationals and the nationals of the covenant-breaking State, and the prevention of all financial, commercial or personal intercourse between the nationals of the covenant-breaking State and the nationals of any other State whether a member of the League or not.' If words have any meaning the members must pledge themselves to maintain the present world boundaries despite the ominous fact that these boundaries are recognised in all responsible political circles to be a bar to permanent world peace. Article XIX certainly holds out a better hope. The members may advise the reconsideration of the treaties if they have become impracticable or endanger the peace of the world. It is significant, however, that not one member has yet ventured to whisper the word 'Revise'. The League has wrought great things, but there are even greater victories within its reach. It must cease, however, to be a political weapon and must be spiritualised. Where will you get that driving power? Democracy? It is itself threatened with doom because it lacks a spiritual dynamic. No, we must have something more. Nothing can avail us save a universal disinterested power which in every land will nurture those impulses towards fellowship wherein alone lies the hope of world peace. The Church is a stern necessity in international affairs.

"It is a commonplace that industry is in the throes of a

crisis. It has been ruined by what is called 'pecuniary self-interest'. Every factory is an armed camp, and the community inevitably suffers. Industry must choose between anarchy and co-operation. Its salvation rests in disinterested service. But, without the dynamic of the Church that hope is vain. Wherever you turn in human affairs you find disillusionment. Give the Church a new chance. She has failed—none know it better than we do; she has failed because she has been less catholic, than national, less Christian than patriotic. Let her rise on the wings of faith and love and a new song will ring out on the night of human woe. I believe in the Church. From age to age she endures on, refusing to despair—content, not with rescuing an individual here and there, but with nothing less than the redemption of humanity itself. Let us get out of the ruts of traditionalism and formalism and burn with a new passion to serve her. Many things must go. Our service, methods, even the buildings themselves are out-worn with time—they have lost their romance and thrill. Let us stand again under the open skies where we may feel the kiss of the breeze upon our cheeks until we thrill to the assurance that she can renew her youth in the womb of human need. Reality and romance are the feet by which she traverses the hurrying avenues of life.

"Finally, recall the message of the Church. A series of hints will never do. Our message must be positive, experimental and redemptive, and it must be fertilised by a fresh movement of the Spirit. There are two kinds of surgeons. The one knows no remedy save the knife—his ideal figure is one sans appendix, sans tonsils, sans teeth, sans everything. It was such a surgeon who said, 'The operation was a splendid success, the patient died.' The other conceives his life's task in the terms of healing. The difference between them is not that the one is better trained than the other but that he is touched with the spirit of our suffering humanity. That is how I conceive our message. Positive, tender, a harbinger of joy to those whose every hope has gone.

"(a) It must be big enough to embrace the needs of this new world. If we trace the history of our faith we shall find the tide is at the full when four facts are emphasised. They are the Personality of God, the Worth of Men, the Reality of Sin and the Revolutionary Character of the Gospel. Attenuate any of these and you dim the wonder of our message. It is what men mean by the word 'Jesus'. The history of religion is the record of the development of these gladdening assurances. Would that we might stake everything upon them. The personality of God has been merged into the flowing movement of life—so how can men pray? Faith in the worth of man evokes a cynical amusement—so how can they hope? Sin is so evacuated of meaning that the very word has become unfamiliar, whilst the heroism of the Gospel is mocked by our pathetic ineffectiveness—the Cross itself is a mere pendant for our watch-chains. Would we were swept into a new experience of the Gospel. Humanity is starved, the real self is perishing; we have the food for which men are hungering. Why not, in the exuberance of your love, break the bread of life for men? Nothing less than the utmost will satisfy the deep yearnings of their souls.

"(b) It must be heroic enough to fire the imagination of this new world. Man thrills to the adventure. Sophocles knew that.

> 'Much there is passing strange,
> Nothing surpassing mankind;
> He it is who loves to range
> Over the ocean hoar,
> Though the surge's roar
> South winds raging behind'

That is the stuff of human nature. How we misinterpret it. We emphasise security, man seeks danger; we talk of peace while he tingles to the music of battle; we woo him with the joys of serenity, he knows the finer joys of sacrifice. He is willing to die for a great end, whilst our presentation of the Gospel seems to him a futile insurance, inspired by a pathetic fear of the hereafter. The intrusion of self despoils our music, but Jesus said, that 'self' must wither and die. That is the difference between us and Him. He never compromised. He made everything difficult. He was defeated—and from the agony of His defeat was born the power that redeems the world. It is the heroic note we must sound out and in the Cross we have a symbol of the mightiest heroism that ever appeared in the arena of time.

"I know that the abiding needs of the heart remain. Sin, suffering and fear of death. If we do not minister to those needs, then others will. We should never forgive ourselves if we let our fellows down. But I bleed for the recovery of the heroic note. Let us venture everything—for His dear sake. When in the forgetfulness of self we make that venture, youth will rally to us again, for the music of heroic deeds abides as a diapason in the heart.

"(c) It must be passionate enough to satisfy the yearnings of this new age. A good deal of preaching leaves me cold. The fact is we don't preach, we converse, and the conversation is a monologue. The preacher's greatest asset is intensity. However poor your equipment may be, if you have something to say, something minted in the deeps of your own experience, men will hear you.

"We have taken a long journey, but I trust the Master has walked with us. How truly envious our fortunes are. We have been called to serve in no mean hour. 'Now God be thanked, who has matched us with His hour, and caught our youth, and wakened us from sleeping'. We have been called to serve that Church whom 'time cannot wither, nor custom stale her infinite variety', to demonstrate the supremacy of that love which was vindicated on the Cross. Love is everything. Call it affinity if you will, it is only another name for love. We take our stand on love. Christina Rossetti has uttered the final word:

'What is the beginning? Love.
What the course? Love still.
What the goal? The goal is love on the happy hill.
Is there nothing, then, but love, search we sky or earth?
There is nothing out of love hath perpetual worth;
All things flag but only love, all things fail or flee.
There is nothing left but love worthy you and me.' "

Although some of the language is a little flowery it is interesting to see how many contemporary problems are touched on:—
the disintegration of external authority
the annihilation of space
the potentialities of atomic energy
the achievements of medical science
the non-inevitability of progress
the impotence of the church
the unimportance of existing church buildings
the message of humanism
the loss of Biblical authority
the narrowness of denominationalism
the struggle between capital and labour

Epstein's sculpture is commented on favourably, poets are quoted from and the old non-conformist Liberal alliance rears its declining head in the allusion to the League of Nations and the Treaty of Versailles. An easy revivalist campaign is not favoured—four essentials must be emphasised, the peronality of God, the worth of men, the reality of sin and the revolutionary character of the gospel.

This was no narrow-minded fundamentalist, no bigoted Puritan, no hot gospeller with a quick sell relying on an appeal to the emotions, but the effort of a largely self-educated man to confront courageously the biggest problems of his time and our time.

Throughout the twenties he preached and preached in English and Welsh, at Myrtle Street and all over Lancashire

c*

and North Wales. The congregations improved, the income of the church grew, new seating was installed, printed forms of service and hymns for each Sunday were in use. There was a salaried organist and a professional quartet of men and women to lead the choir. On Sunday afternoons the church was full of hundreds of boys and girls at a service where cinema techniques were used and a large screen occupied the place of honour about the pulpit. On several occasions my father was invited to broadcast and I can remember hurrying home with my mother from the evening service to hear his voice. Under the enlightened Bishop David, the Anglican Bishop of Liverpool, whose supporting clergy at the time included Canon Raven, he and other Free Churchmen were invited to speak in the Cathedral—Liverpool in this respect being decades ahead of its times. He became President of the local Free Church Council, which had under its jurisdiction about three hundred churches. Everything seemed to be going well for him and his Church.

Through the eyes of a child it all looked rather different. I felt, rather than knew, and I felt correctly, that my father was a man of some importance and I derived some prestige from being his son just as I did from having an uncle who won the last V.C. in the 1914–18 war. (It was a bitter disappointment when I discovered that he wasn't a genuine uncle but only a friend of my mother and father.) Quite apart from the prestige there were the more solid advantages which I derived from the standard of living which my father could afford— the size of the house, the domestic servant, the car when cars were still rarities (the only other car in the road was owned by our Bank Manager), the food, clothing and schooling. But these I took for granted although I noticed that many of the children who attended Sunday School with me had neither shoes nor stockings—what I also noticed was that members of my father's congregation were rather apt to make a fuss of me which was sometimes pleasurable and sometimes not. I did appreciate some of the more tangible signs of their attention such as a regular fortnightly present of home-made fudge slipped into our pew on a Sunday evening and the Christmas gift of a gold half sovereign from the church Treasurer and lesser offerings of shillings and half crowns throughout the year. Additional presents in kind at Christmas were always welcome including on one occasion a very fine car—unfortunately my parents had bought me a better one which in the interests of internal church politics had to be returned. Satisfaction could also be obtained from a never ending succession of high teas in the homes of church members when I could usually get on quietly with stuffing myself while the grown-ups chattered away.

I liked having my father around and I liked the books all over the place.

But these pleasures had to be paid for and at times I felt the price was rather heavy. Church three times on Sunday—morning service, afternoon Sunday School and evening service; having to wear my best suit on Sundays; having to keep quiet when my father was working; being for ever dragged along to sales of work and bazaars when the staple diet was salmon-paste sandwiches.

There was even one occasion when at some church function I was forced to appear dressed as Cupid complete with bow and arrow much to the delight of the cohorts of old ladies present. Fortunately none of my friends was there but it is difficult looking back to decide which was more incongruous, Cupid in a Baptist church hall or myself as Cupid. But above all there was the feeling that Sunday the Sabbath was a different day, when the very air became more holy.

In his autobiography, "My Dear Timothy," Victor Gollancz has described the horrors of the Jewish Sabbath in his own family—no riding, smoking, writing, painting, piano playing. sometimes owing to bad weather he writes, "My father would announce to my—I was going to say 'to my relief', but that is a feeble expression, for often I would hop from foot to foot in an ecstasy of delight—my father would announce 'No Synagogue today'. (Not to go would be a pity: to go in a vehicle would be unthinkable)."

Speaking of the Day of Atonement he writes:—
"Every year as Kippur approached I began to feel something
I find it very difficult to express: something midway between
apprehension and malaise: something concerned with the
body, but spiritual, in a groping sort of way, as well: something stemming at the same time, from the reasoning faculty
and power of judgment. The more inescapable it became, as
the days passed by, that Kippur would eventually arrive, the
more eagerly I looked forward to the moment when it would
at last have gone by and be behind me; and the relief I
envisaged as awaiting me at the end of it was the relief of
not stifling, the relief of drawing breath again, the relief of
no longer having steel bands on me, the relief of being free.
I could not have said at the time, what I meant by this freedom, but I think I understand it now."

For me every Sunday was a Day of Atonement.

When many years later I read Churchill's "My Early Life",
the following passage struck a responsive chord:—

"Even in the holidays I always had to go once a week to
Church, and at Harrow there were three services every Sunday, besides morning and evening prayer throughout the
week. All this was very good. I accumulated so fine a surplus
in the Bank of Observance that I have been drawing confi-
dently upon it ever since. Weddings, christenings and
funerals have brought in a steady annual income, and I have
never made too close enquiries about the state of my account.
It might well even be that I should find an overdraft. But
now in the bright days of youth my attendances were well
ahead of the Sundays."

If asked at the time I too would have felt the same, and the
great man got away with once on Sundays, unlike Sir Henry
Jones who wrote that he was in Chapel practically every night
of the week except Saturdays and on Sundays "from 8.30 a.m.
to 9.30 a.m. there was the young men's prayer-meeting which
we attended after a very hasty breakfast. From 9.30 a.m. to
10.30 a.m. there was the public prayer-meeting or a sermon—

At 12 noon we had our one meat dinner of the week . . .
At 1 p.m. there was the young men's reading class in which
we sat till the Sunday school opened at 2 p.m. At 3.30 p.m.
the school closed; at 4 p.m. we had tea; from 5 p.m. to
6 p.m. there was the singing meeting; at 6 p.m. the Chapel
filled for the sermon which usually lasted till 7.30 p.m.;
from 7.30 p.m. to 8 p.m. there was the meeting of the church
members *only*, mere adherents having gone home. Did ever
a boy have a better chance of being either very religious, or
very much the opposite? But so far as I know I was neither
. . ."

Although, if I fared worse than Churchill, I was far better
off than Sir Henry Jones, it seemed to me that the system
under which I was brought up favoured the Minister rather
than the Minister's son. After all it was his job to go to
church and on Monday mornings he could play golf while
I had to go to school. Even now I can never shake off the
feeling that Sunday is different.

My father's father stopped smoking his pipe before he
went to bed on Saturdays and did not smoke again until
Monday morning. My father did not stop smoking—indeed
his habit of having a cigarette almost immediately after a
service was over sometimes gave offence to church members.
Now we have the day devoted to late mornings in bed,
wallowing in the Sunday papers, drinks before lunch, outings,
hobbies, sport and visiting relations. Cinemas and entertainments are open. We can choose between watching Royalty
playing polo and professionals playing Sunday cricket and as
we retire into our own privacy for Sunday evening we
occasionally hear, if the wind is in a certain quarter, that
glorious sound of old, the rise and fall of church bells in the
valley. As we go into the house—

> The radiant morn hath passed away
> And spent too soon her golden store
> The shadows of departing day
> Creep on once more

And I feel a ghastly black sad depression recurring almost every Sunday evening—it filters through the windows with the sound of the bells and the shadows of the sinking sun, a yearning for what once was and can never be again.

> Once more 'tis eventide, and we
> Oppressed with various ills draw near;
> What if thy Form we cannot see?
> We know and feel that thou art here.
>
> O Saviour Christ, our woes dispel;
> For some are sick and some are sad,
> And some have never loved thee well,
> And some have lost the love they had.
>
> Thy touch has still its ancient power;
> No word from Thee can fruitless fall;
> Hear in this solemn evening hour,
> And in Thy mercy heal us all.

What if thy Form we cannot see? Thy touch has still its ancient power?

My anguish increased a thousandfold from having lost the love I had, I contemplate the blackness of the night alone and shuddering clutch for comfort the living, decaying flesh of my wife. Childhood is simultaneously only a moment ago, and, yet, far more distant than fifty years.

"Cocky, self-assertive, . . . an apparent self confidence, even verging on arrogance, . . . the noisiest and most ebullient children I have ever come across . . . artful Dodgers, that's the kind of boy you'll find here"—writes Graham Turner of Liverpool in "The North Country" published in 1967.

It was only shortly before he died that I dared to tell my father about the smoking—well—he probably guessed about the smoking because he himself started at the same age—seven or eight, but I mean the smoking I'm just going to tell you about.

Having begun smoking cigarettes as far as I can now recollect in the sand dunes at what was then known as St.

Annes on Sea, but I believe is now called Lytham St. Annes, I soon progressed to a pipe and dead tree leaves in the alley way or entry at the back of our house. I found cigarettes of virginia tobacco preferable—problem—where did one get them and where could one smoke them in greatest comfort and safety? Answer—one got them by taking one or two at a time from the drawers of the desk in my father's study at home and one smoked in comfort in his vestry at Myrtle Street Baptist Church before Sunday School. It was also safe because the Sunday School was held in the vast cavernous basement underneath the church whilst his vestry was on the ground floor. For weeks therefore I had a puff or two in the quiet seclusion of his vestry before proceeding down-stairs to take part for the umpteenth time in the children's hymns, bible stories and singularly unsuccessful artistic efforts with plasticine and sand trays, and by then I had had enough of plasticine and sand trays to last me the rest of my life. I don't know how long this would have gone on had it not been for the fact that one Sunday afternoon I was discovered smoking by one of my father's Deacons who also helped in the Sunday School. I then realised with the blinding revelation which came to Paul on the road to Damascus that should my father get to know he was unlikely to regard the matter with amusement. I was terrified and suffered agonies for weeks wondering whether or not the Deacon would tell my father. He never did—but the incident cured me of smoking for some years and I didn't take it up again seriously till the age of twelve when I was living away from home.

Not only was I terrified of what my father would do to me if he found out—I also had a very bad conscience. I knew only too well the story of Joddy and the peppermints which was one of my father's favourite children's addresses. It went something like this—

"A few weeks ago I was out walking with a friend when I suddenly remembered that it was my wife's birthday a day or two ahead. We happened to be passing a flower shop at the time and in the window were some flowering bulbs in pots. So I went in and bought one and gave it to my wife on her birthday. A day or two later the flower died—I emptied the flower pot and cut open the bulb and there in the bulb was a canker worm.

"It reminded me of the story of Joddy and the peppermints —do you like peppermints—I like them very much—my mother used to give me peppermints during the sermon—one every ten minutes and I usually got four or five. Joddy liked peppermints too.

"One day when he was staying with his grandmother she went out shopping—and before she went out she said to him—'Be a good boy while I'm out Joddy and don't touch anything'. So Joddy settled down to read a book—but his granny was rather a long time and Joddy got bored and began to look around the room. There was a small metal box on a table in which Joddy's granny kept some peppermints because she suffered from indigestion. Joddy thought there could be no harm in just looking inside the box although he never had any intention of actually taking a peppermint. So he opened the box and then thought that he might just as well count the peppermints to see how many there were. One, two, three, four, five, six, seven, eight, nine, ten, eleven. Joddy wondered whether he had counted correctly so he thought he better count them again—one, two, three, four, five, six, seven, eight, nine, ten—that's funny thought Joddy —I better check up—one, two, three, four, five, six, seven, eight, nine. And each time Joddy counted them there were less peppermints until after a while there were none. And when there were no peppermints Joddy began to get a little worried. Soon his granny would be home—should he admit what he had done, should he keep silent, what should he say if she asked him what had happened to her peppermints?

"I'm sorry to say that Joddy decided, as many of us would have done, to say nothing. A few days later he went home to his mother and father. And then a funny thing happened. He no longer wanted to play his usual games. He couldn't settle down to reading. He seemed to have lost his appetite. Instead of being cheerful and noisy he was sad and silent. He looked as though he were sickening for some illness. His mother became quite worried about him.

"You see, children—(pause) the canker worm had got into the heart of Joddy."

Now I realised the canker worm had got into my heart too—I'm afraid it is still there and has been growing ever since.

If only I had known then what Spurgeon had said about smoking in a letter to the Daily Telegraph in 1874 following on a controversy which has arisen over his having spoken in the pulpit of smoking a cigar to the glory of God.

"I demur altogether and most positively to the statement that to smoke tobacco is in itself a sin. It may become so, as any other indifferent action may, but as an action it is no sin. Together with hundreds of thousands of my fellow Christians I have smoked and, with them, I am under the condemnation of living in habitual sin, if certain accusers are to be believed. As I would not knowingly live in the smallest violation of the law of God, and sin is the transgression of the law, I will not own to sin when I am not conscious of it. There is growing up in society a Pharisaic system which adds to the commands of God the precepts of men; to that system I will not yield for an hour. The preservation of my libery may bring upon me the upbraidings of many good men, and the sneers of the self-righteous; but I shall endure both with serenity, so long as I feel clear in my conscience before God. The expression 'smoking to the glory of God' standing alone has an ill sound, and I do not justify it; but in the sense in which I employed it I still stand to it. No Christian should do anything in which he cannot glorify God, and this may be done, according to scripture, in eating and drinking and the common actions of life. When I have found intense pain relieved, a weary brain soothed, and calm refreshing sleep obtained by a cigar, I have felt grateful to God and have blessed His name: this is what I meant, and by no means did I use sacred words triflingly . . . I am told that my open avowal will lessen my influence, and my reply is that if I have gained any influence through being thought different from what I am, I have no wish to retain it. I will do nothing upon the sly, and nothing about which I have a doubt."

No, on second thoughts, Spurgeon's words would not have helped me to defend myself. By no stretch of the imagination could I have argued that I was smoking to the glory of God even though I was using the vestry. And it was "upon the sly".

So far I have written of the public figure—what of the private face, what was it like at home with this well-known and respected preacher?

To pass the time my mother would sometimes play the piano and my father sing songs such as "Devon, glorious Devon", "Because", "Trees" and other favourite solo pieces of the late Victorian and Edwardian eras, but then family entertainments were gradually killed off by the wireless and gramophone. My father could not compete with Ernest Lough's "O For the Wings of a Dove" or Dame Clara Butt's "Abide with me". Only the pictures on the walls lingered on as reminders of an earlier epoch—George Frederick Watt's "Hope of the World", Rosetti's "Behold the Handmaiden of the Lord", Millet's "The Angelus" and Walter Dendy Sadler's "Thursday"—the famous picture of monks fishing. I liked the monks, didn't mind the peasants in the Angelus, was puzzled by the Hope of the World and never warmed to the Handmaiden of the Lord. Meanwhile in school history books we had "When did you last see your father?", "The Retreat from Moscow" and "Napoleon on board H.M.S. 'Bellerophon' ".

Grace was said before meals and prayers before going to bed. At first I knelt at my mothers's knees and went through the kind of ritual immortalised by A. A. Milne:—

"Gentle Jesus, meek and mild,
Look upon a little child,
Pity my simplicity,
Suffer me to come to thee."

As, warm from the bath, I nosed my way into my mother's dress and thighs I was usually quite happy to go through the performance and did not resent it as a waste of time. Whether I understood the meaning of the word "suffer" I rather doubt but certainly the picture of a meek and mild Jesus was strongly reinforced at Sunday School where there was always prominently displayed a coloured reproduction of an attractive young white Englishman with a beard, dressed in a white nightshirt surrounded by a group of revoltingly good little children of various nationalities looking up at him adoringly. That picture used to follow me around from church to church. It obviously influenced many men of my generation very powerfully. When in the sixties and seventies long hair and beards returned to fashion among the young, their fathers' first reaction was to recoil in horror from the living representation of Jesus Christ on which they had been brought up as children. "Jesus Christ!" they said, "they look exactly like Jesus Christ".

The habit of saying prayers before going to bed was so deeply ingrained that it lasted until I went to boarding school. I was rather frightened about kneeling and saying them there but I got away with it. The fact that I was rather big for my age and could beat anyone in the year above me may have protected me.

On Saturday afternoons my father used to take me to watch Liverpool or Everton playing soccer where I enjoyed looking at the crowd almost as much as seeing Dixie Dean head another goal. It seemed odd that if a home team man was tackled it was always a foul but not when the reverse applied. In Sefton Park, there were old men to watch playing marbles, ducks to feed, a statue of Peter Pan, a floating model of Captain Hook's pirate ship, an aviary and a Palm House. At the Pier Head were the ferry boats and the large Atlantic liners and sometimes my father would say prayers in the cabin for departing passengers. However it was worth ten minutes kneeling for a chance to wander round and be taken down the vast engine room. Sometimes we went for a trip on the overhead railway looking down on dock after dock.

Once a year the Lord Mayor and his train visited the church for a special service. Once a year the Liverpool students held their Rag Day and very good it was with floats of various descriptions. In the winter there was skating and sliding in the parks, the Christmas decorations in the shops and on one occasion the Church's silver band came to play especially for me on Christmas Eve. Unfortunately I never heard them as I was asleep and did not wake up.

Liverpool was a wonderfully entertaining place for a child to be brought up in—if the child was lucky enough to be born in a middle class home—much more interesting than the commuterland in which my children have been reared. But even so a holiday in London was a thrill. It began with the open upper deck of the buses but the climax was the zoo. To start with there was that smell, and then the incredible size of the elephants' droppings, the baboon's bare behinds (what would they get up to next?) the rides on the llamas and the elephants and then the giraffe house. I liked the giraffes but my pleasure was increased many times when I found one whose name was Mordecai—I pointed it out to my father. He was not amused.

Writing in The Times on the 21st December 1970 Trevor Fishlock said:—

"The growth of the chapel movement in the nineteenth and early twentieth centuries created a fashion for biblical names. Methuselah Jones and Obadiah Evans were well known miners' leaders, and many parents brightened Jones with Shadrack, Mordecai, Moses and Joshua."

My father was given the names Samuel Mordecai. He detested both of them, as well he might. Whenever possible he tried to get by with using initials only. On one occasion in a sermon he referred to Mordecai as "an unhappy individual of a still more unhappy name." But though he might be embarrassed by his names my father was never embarrassed by his dress after he reached Liverpool. His church Treasurer was a first class tailor named Amos Quemby and whenever Quemby thought my father was letting him down he told him to come in and get a new suit. I have in front of me a letter from Amos Quemby to my father written in 1935, the letter head of which reads:—

Quemby and Simpson
(Late Simpson & Sons, York & Scarboro')
Riding Breeches, Motor outfits,
       Liveries

35 North John Street,
  Corner of Matthew St.,
    Liverpool.

Although he didn't run to riding breeches, motor outfits or liveries, my father was much better dressed than his son has ever been—but dress then was much more important than it is now. It was a kind of social camouflage outside the home.

It was the custom at Myrtle Street Baptist Church for the collection to be taken on open wooden platters. From time to time other modes of collection was discussed. The Treasurer's attitude was always the same. Anyone could know what he gave and he was going to know what everyone else gave. The use of the wooden platters continued. The Treasurer obviously agreed with Hugh Stowell Brown who wrote:—

"But really there are some people who don't deserve the protection afforded by the rule of secret alms-giving; people who may well not let their left hand know what their right hand doeth, lest their left hand should be utterly ashamed of their right hand's miserable meanness;—'that thine alms may be in secret!—yes! yes!' For shame's sake let it be in secret

. . . and sometimes the alms is so entirely in secret that God Himself does not see it, because there is none. In the matter of church and chapel collections, boxes and still more those new-fangled nuisances, bags at the ends of long sticks, afford fine cover for meanness and lies. They are a direct encouragement of shabby and untruthful practices against God and man, and, believing that ostentation is a far less sin than fraud, we give the palm to a mode of collection that we have seen in the Staffordshire Potteries, as incomparably the best: Here each collector has two dinner plates, one of which he sends along the pews in succession, while into the other he pours in succession what each pew gives. It is only the generous giver that deserves the protection of secrecy; the shabby people, who substitute half-pence for shillings, and pennies for half-crowns, are treated as they deserve, when all such protection being denied, they are compelled for shame's sake to give decently, or to appear openly in all their nasty stinginess and greed."

The Treasurer's wife was deaf and the only lady I have come across with an ear trumpet. The skill with which she manipulated this weapon made an early and lasting impression on me. She had a formidable presence, spoke in a loud voice and turned the mouth of the trumpet towards the person with whom she wished to converse. The combination of her personality, voice and hearing aid gave her complete domination over any gathering at which she was present and tended to outflank and terrify my somewhat timid mother. In the silent struggle which developed over the years between the Minister's wife and the Treasurer's wife as to who was to run the women's church activities, my mother's youth proved no match for the older lady's toughness and generally superior strategy. Many a battle was fought in committee meetings to organise bazaars, sales of work and other fund-raising activities and many a time my mother retired bleeding to her corner where my father acting as her second, flapped towels at her, and applied spiritual and possibly physical massage to heal the cuts and bruises to her pride.

If any member of the women's liberation movement should have chanced to read so far, she might well feel that in ignoring so greatly the role of my mother I was providing ample evidence of the need for a fundamental change in the relationships between the roles of the sexes in the home. Ours was certainly a male-dominated family. We started off by being two to one and as I grew older the interests of my father and myself in conversation and books tended more and more to exclude my mother. Starting by being brought up in a world in which it was beneath male dignity to do things like washing up, being a dominant personality and eight years older than his wife, my father never lifted a finger to do any domestic chore and I gladly followed his example. My mother was expected to do everything—all the shopping, cooking, house cleaning and mending; all the laundry and ironing. She even fetched his books from the library and he was not pleased if she brought a book home which he had read before. Food, and good food, was expected in time, and, if it was not up to his very high standards, was loudly commented on by my father. On one occasion he accompanied his words by action and threw the food across the table at her. I can still recall, over an interval of forty five years, the bewilderment and sickening shock I felt, as he ranted and raved and stormed out of the room leaving my mother sobbing.

Her difficulties as a cook were not eased by my father's long series of most peculiar diets, which he insisted on following with the utmost strictness and inconvenience to all for weeks or months. Then there would be a switch to a new diet, which was going to be equally life-saving or enhancing and equally troublesome to my mother. He also expected to be, and was, waited on with endless cups of tea, before breakfast, at breakfast, for elevenses, after the midday meal, again in the afternoon and yet again at about ten o'clock at night. He had about twelve or thirteen cups a day and his stomach must have been so lined with tannin that it probably explained why he was always suffering from indigestion. He went on his diets because of the indigestion and he drank so much tea because of the monotony of the diets.

Apart from acting as a general dogsbody and bottle-washer my mother was expected to listen to his sermons in rehearsal, play hymn tunes on the piano for him when he was choosing the next Sunday's hymns, sew and stitch for sales of work and bazaars, attend all church services and weekday meetings and remember everyone's name and all about them. In all these functions which she fulfilled impeccably, she was thereby releasing my father from the mundane problems of daily life and providing him with the necessary time to think of higher things. Like Mary my father had chosen the good part—my mother was poor old Martha. Despite the fact that he was so dependent on her in so many ways he was often contemptuous of her, and what little self-confidence she may have started with when they married was rapidly knocked out of her so that she tended to flap—as well she might—in a family crisis. She was even supervised when she went out to buy clothes and was so criticised when trying to drive a car that she gave up after a few months.

If my father was particularly displeased with some real or imagined error on her part he would sulk for days—sending her to Coventry and creating the kind of atmosphere inside a home which can be felt as soon as one enters the front door. In short, this Christian Minister behaved in a way which would probably have enabled my mother to divorce him on the grounds of cruelty if the thought of divorce had even crossed her mind—and as a divorce lawyer I know what I am talking about. He was bad-tempered, selfish, proud and a little vain. John Stuart Mill has written:—

"If the family in its best form is, as it is often said to be, a school of sympathy, tenderness and loving forgetfulness of self, it is still oftener as repects its chief, a school of wilfulness, overbearingness, unbounded selfish indulgence, and a double-dyed and idealised selfishness, of which sacrifice itself is only a particular form: the care for the wife and children being only care for them as parts of the man's own interests and belongings, and their individual happiness being immolated in every shape to his smallest preferences."

He sounds pretty ghastly, doesn't he? And yet for so much of the time he could be, and was, sympathetic, charming, always generous and always with you in trouble. He may, like Christmas Evans and many other less famous preachers, not always have practised the words at home which he preached at church, but then he might have been a great deal worse without his religion. Mary McCarthy has said that Christianity makes good people better and bad people worse—one of those clever sayings which have an instant appeal. But most people are not good people or bad people—they are both—and thanks to his religion when my father did something wrong he felt ashamed, but not ashamed to pray for forgiveness.

Throughout my life I knew that if I had sent him a telegram "Am in bad trouble. Please cut off your right arm and send it to me" his right arm would have arrived as quickly as possible. And my mother and all the family knew that in any crisis he was the one to turn to, that when the chips were down the whole of his strength, integrity, and love were at your service—a difficult man to live with but a man to rely on in trouble.

As for my mother, bullied by my father, frequently ill because she had only one kidney, soft hearted, too soft with him and too soft with me, always overworked, she had a much more interesting and worthwhile life than many of today's home-locked, restless, bored and better educated wives. She did not merely run on her own a male dominated home and save pennies by bottling, pickling, jam making and baking. Visitors to the home were frequent and she had a full role to play in the life of the church. She might have been happier with a less dominating husband but she had no problem about combining a career with a home and family.

Meanwhile for the public figure things were not going so well for my father and Myrtle Street Baptist Church. He was swimming against too many tides. His was a predominantly middle class and lower middle class congregation and his members were moving out to the suburbs. They no longer relished crossing the Mersey by ferryboat or long tram rides to church. Few as yet had cars. A symptomatic battle over the opening of cinemas on Sundays was fought and lost. The novelty of the new Minister's impact had long faded. Congregations declined, church collections fell—should the Church move out to the suburbs?

Years before Hugh Stowell Brown had forseen the danger:—

"Twenty years ago . . . the town itself did not spread over so vast a space; comparatively few dwelt at a distance of more than a mile from the chapel. The centrifugal force has become so great, and dissenters have got on so well in the world, that I could speak of many who once lived within ten minutes' walk of the chapel who now reside far off in the suburbs."

To the older deacons any thought of moving was unbearable. To ask them to acquiesce willingly in the obliteration of the building in which they had worshipped since they were boys was asking for more than a sacrifice of flesh and blood. Ever greater efforts were made to raise money—individual appeals were sent out all over the country, but the church was melting away. The cynicism of the Twenties after the immediate post war hopes of a land fit for heroes to live in was a powerful ally of those intellectual movements which by now had worked themselves down from their lofty Victorian pioneers to a lower level. Echoes of the Huxley-Wilberforce debate were reaching out. Material comfort seemed a more attractive immediate proposition than spiritual solace. Under the strain my father broke.

"When I lie down, I say, when shall I arise, and the night

be gone? and I am full of tossings to and fro unto the dawning of the day.

"My flesh is clothed with worms and clods of dust; my skin is broken and become loathsome."

For three months the skin rash over the whole of my father's body was so bad that he did not go to bed. At night he anointed himself with calamine and wrapped himself in lint gauze to prevent his fingers tearing at his skin until the blood flowed. He sat in a chair. After a year or so the worst was over, but never again as long as he lived could he have a hot bath, or swim. The doctors told him how lucky he was to have a skin eruption instead of a nervous breakdown. The following extracts are taken from "The Highroad" of December 1931:—

"Free churchmen of Liverpool noted with surprise and regret that the Rev. S. M. Morris had informed his congregation, Myrtle Street Baptist Church, that he was concluding his Ministry among them at the end of the year. At the November Meeting of the Executive of the Liverpool Free Church Centre a letter was received from Mr. Morris resigning his position on that Committee and on the Secretarial Board. The intimation was very unwelcome as the Centre owes much to him . . . the main foundation for the success (of the Centre) lay in his statesmanship and business capacity, in his enthusiasm, courage and pertinacity, and his readiness to give time and thought alike to main issues and smaller details.

"He is a convinced and ardent Free Churchman, who believes that the Free Churches have a distinctive work to do and a distinctive witness to bear in our land.

"Mr. Morris is in great demand for special services and lectures up and down the country. Whenever on public occasions he has represented the Free Churches in pulpit or platform it has been with credit to himself and great satisfaction to his people. In addition to his double term as President he served the Centre and the Free Church Community it represents on the National Free Church Council Executive and on the advisory Board of the British Broadcast Committee.

"Mr. Morris possesses a gift of fervid, nay perfervid eloquence, and both his prepared and extempore utterances are marked by richness of diction, fluency of utterance, fertility and freshness of thought and manifestly have basis of wide and careful reading.

"We suppose Mr. Morris has found the difficulty of carrying on a down-town church with a widely scattered membership in a building vastly too large as modern congregations go, and without any endowment to make easy the financing of the work . . .

"Mr. Morris is still young, and full of zest and vitality, and it will not be long before we hear he has taken up, and is carying forward some important work for the Kingdom and Master elsewhere. He carries with him the good wishes and gratitude of many Free Church men and women."

It is a fine tribute which I like to think was deserved, but although he was only forty four years old he had already reached the peak of his achievement for the "work of the Kingdom" and was on the way down hill and into the shadows. It was true, however, that he would be heard of again. Within two years he had preached a rocket of a sermon which burst into brief starlight splendour before the night finally descended.

A few years after he left Liverpool, Myrtle Street Baptist Church was sold and demolished. Only the statue of Hugh Stowell Brown remained. The site was acquired for a hospital, on the assumption, which has proved correct, that men of the Twentieth Century would travel further to save their bodies than to save their souls.

Lead, kindly Light, amid the encircling gloom,
  Lead Thou me on;
The night is dark, and I am far from home,
  Lead Thou me on.
Keep Thou my feet; I do not ask to see
The distant scene; one step enough for me.

I was not ever thus, nor pray'd that Thou
  Shouldst lead me on;
I loved to choose and see my path; but now
  Lead Thou me on.
I loved the garish day, and, spite of fears,
Pride ruled my will: remember not past years.

So long Thy power hath blest me, sure it still
  Will lead me on,
O'er moor and fen, o'er crag and torrent, till
  The night is gone;
And with the morn those Angel faces smile,
Which I have loved long since, and lost awhile.

J. H. NEWMAN

Four

A crazy comedy night at Clacton-on-Sea

His next church was at Clacton-on-Sea—and apart from the fact that they are both on the coast it would be difficult to find two more contrasting places than Liverpool and Clacton. Liverpool black, dirty, energetic, large, racially mixed, intellectually awake where the warm western wind brought rain, rain, rain, and Clacton clean, narrow-minded, sunny with an icy wind blowing straight from Siberia. The church was big, seating eight or nine hundred people, and for two months in the year in the season it was full. But the season on the East Coast is short and for most of the year the women who kept boarding houses and who were suspected by the summer visitors of being fleecing witches were counting every penny with nothing to do except gossip. The town was full of retired elderly couples also with nothing to do. There was no industry. There were almost no young people. A few intrepid commuters went to London and back daily from the cleanest railway station I've ever seen in England—a station such as one finds in Switzerland.

Into the old bottle of this church my father poured the new wine of his preaching but he soon had to water the wine. The intellectual horizons of the Baptists of Clacton-on-Sea were narrow indeed. No longer could my father make use of his wide reading—the message had to be premasticated and chewed to tastelessness before being passed on to the sheep. But my mother was well for the first time in years. My father had golf and a garden to delight in, and in the summer when the church was full he could still feel the old intoxication of the preacher's power.

As a result of the move from Liverpool to Clacton and the need to get a new school quickly I was sent to live with my mother's parents at South Woodford. At the time South Woodford was on the edge of the Great Wen and across the road where my grandparents lived the fields began. They lived in a house built probably in the eighteen nineties; two rooms and a small kitchen downstairs, three bedrooms upstairs, almost no front garden but a narrow strip stretching back behind. No house could be seen from the back bedroom windows and in the spring the sea of apple, plum and pear blossom washed over and obliterated boundary fences.

Milk was delivered in a horse drawn milk float and the milkman was killed one day when the horse reared and flung him backwards off the float. Vegetables were also sold from the horse and cart. There was so much horse traffic up and down the road that there was an inexhaustible supply of horse dung for the garden collected by small boys and brought to the door. My grandmother also bought vegetables from a greengrocer's in George Lane. I used to like going with her as the greengrocer was always kind to me. My grandmother wrote out the bill for him as he couldn't write.

The front room downstairs of my grandparents' house contained the most uncomfortable seats I have ever come across, and that includes the experience of a wide variety of chapels. The armchairs and settee consisted of a frame of the most elaborately carved wood with knobs and sharp edges sticking out all over the place. It was as though a very distant disciple of Grinling Gibbons had conceived the suite in a nightmare and executed it while drunk. Here and there one came across an isolated patch of stuffed fabric which was soft only by comparison with the knobs. There were antimacassars on each piece of furniture, lace net and dark green velvet curtains and an aspidistra in a brass pot on a small table in the window. On the walls there were framed texts and dotted about in glass cases one or two stuffed birds. Fortunately the discomfort of the furniture mattered little because the room was only used very occasionally such as at Christmas time. The whole of the living of the house went on in the back room where there were two comfortable chairs. Here there were two pictures one of Vesuvius by Day and the other Vesuvius by Night; a large table covered with a dark green tasselled cloth, several upright chairs, a book case without any books in it, an open fire surrounded by a kind of Chinese Gothic wooden pagoda full of shelves and crannies into each one of which fitted brass pots and brass ornaments, whilst in the hearth with its brass surround were the brass fire irons and a brass toaster. On one side of the hearth was a low cupboard in which my grandfather kept some glasses, which I still use, a bottle of port and a box or two of cigars. From the room one could see into the garden through a small glass conservatory in which there were almost no plants but a whole lot more stuffed birds. In the summer a rose bush covered the roof of the conservatory.

The front bedroom upstairs was occupied by my Great Aunt Gable, then aged eighty-five. There had only been a short interval after my grandmother had stopped looking after her mother before Aunt Gable was taken in and sheltered. She had her breakfast in her bedroom and spent most of the morning going through an elaborate toilet which apart from dressing involved the using of a variety of pins and hairpieces of varying lengths. Her dressing table was a positive armoury of dangerous weapons. She then came downstairs and ate a hearty lunch. My grandmother and my Great Aunt, each with a crochet shawl around her shoulders, would then sleep during the afternoon. Awaking refreshed, Great Aunt Gable was then ready for a large ham and tongue tea to be followed by solo whist, and she loved "The rigour of the game" as much as did old Sarah Battle. After a light supper at about nine thirty of cheese, pickles, tomatoes and probably more ham and tongue she retired to bed. She never took any exercise, ate nearly as much as I did and was as thin as a rake. With her velvet choker concealing the vertical folds of her scrawny neck and her bobbing Adams apple, with her eyes sharp and bright on the cards, with her hair style as elaborate as Marie Antoinette's, this lady who had been born before the Crimean War began was the living embodiment of the Victorian age.

There was a never ending supply of ham and tongue in the house because my grandfather worked in a shop in London Wall where sandwiches were sold for lunch. It was the best ham I have ever tasted and bore no resemblance whatsoever to the insipid muck bearing the same name which today is sold in thin slices from tins. Every morning save Sunday he caught the eight thirty three to Liverpool Street. He was home at about five forty five when he ate a hot dinner which had been kept since the midday meal. In the winter he would then usually sit in the chair and pretend to read a book before going to sleep, although he also sometimes took part in a game of cards or listened to Tommy Handley or Clapham and Dwyer or the Western Brothers or Mabel Constandouros. At ten o'clock he locked up the house, turned out the gas light and, taking his candle, climbed by its flickering flame the creaking stairs to bed, under which was his deed box. Locking up the house was a fairly long procedure as my grandfather was scared of burglars and there were seven or eight different kinds of locks on the front door and several more on the back door. Any burglar could have come through any of the windows in a few moments. In the summer he pottered in his shed and garden and sometimes killed a chicken for my grandmother to gut and cook. His deed-box was full of the papers of small properties which he owned, bonds which he held and wills of which he was executor. On rare occasions when he thought the rest of the family was sleeping he inspected the contents of this box. Apart from burglars he was also very frightened of cars and it took him about five minutes to cross the main road because

D

he looked so carefully and fearfully. He was a typical middle or lower middle class bourgeois or rentier whose interests were bounded by his family, his work, his food and his garden. But this frightened, limited little man had when young sailed in a windjammer to New Zealand, worked there on a sheep farm and continued the voyage round the world under sail. He could remember when East India Dock was a tangled mass of spars, when Epping Forest crept almost to the old gates of the City of London, when Victoria ruled in the land and England was the most powerful country in the world. And when Hitler's bombs came this frightened man refused to leave his home, although he had enough money to move, and no work to keep him and although he was only making a nuisance of himself by staying.

In this household I lived for two and a half years hating my school but loving my grandparents. I read a great deal mostly by candlelight in bed. It would be pleasant for my self-esteem to picture myself as a budding literary genius imbibing early in life intoxicating drafts of English literature, my young mind and soul being enriched and expanded by the glorious inheritance of our language. I did in fact read most of Dickens in an edition which was being issued cheaply by a newspaper in one of those numerous efforts to support a flagging circulation which were were already a feature of the times. But apart from Dickens the literature which appealed to me from eleven to thirteen years of age has not, I think, formed part of the syllabus of university courses in English, although it has been studied in a famous essay by George Orwell and, more extensively in E. S. Turner's marvellous "Boys will be Boys". By then I had moved on from Harry Wharton and Billy Bunter and gradually worked my way through all the Tarzan and Hopalong Cassidy books I could lay my hands on. I also enjoyed, although I was rather ashamed of still enjoying, Skipper, Rover and Wizard. To whet my stirring sexual appetite I had to rely on an occasional smuggled paperback hastily hidden in a drawer. So unpermissive was this kind of literature at the time that although I set out eagerly enough in the quest for further knowledge I was invariably bitterly disappointed, being well able to supply from my own imagination far more erotically stimulating scenes than those described in the magazines on which I had wasted my money.

On Saturday afternoons I watched my uncles playing soccer for a team which had originated as an offspring of the local Baptist Church, or I went to the cinema. One got one's money's worth then. News, Mickey Mouse, two full length films and often a Whurlitzer organ or a brief variety show with people like Billy Cotton and his Band. The programme lasted three to three and a half hours and one emerged with eyes sore and head aching from the hot smoky atmosphere and a stiff neck from looking up at the screen from the cheap seats in front. I was also smoking fairly heavily.

One hot summer night as I lay in bed trying to get to sleep, a noise which I have never heard before or since began to fill the room. It was not as hard or brittle a noise as that of an aeroplane and it was not travelling so fast. It seemed much more menacing because slowly but inexorably the volume increased. I went to the window in time to see the underbelly of a great whale sailing gently overhead through the sky. It was the Graf Zeppelin.

By now I was making my first tentative moves towards escaping from the previous Sunday regime. Sundays in my grandparents' home followed an invariable ritual. Whereas on weekdays my grandfather got up first and lit the coal fire, on Sundays he had breakfast in bed—breakfast consisting of ham sandwiches and tea. My grandmother then went to morning church at George Lane Baptist Church and while she was out my grandfather got up, had a bath and then cooked the Sunday dinner. In the evening he accompanied my grandmother to church. At first I went with my grandmother to church in the morning, alone to Sunday School in the afternoon and with both of then again in the evening. Gradually I succeeded in dropping the Sunday School. Then

I suggested that in the mornings I should go to a small tin tabernacle round the corner which was much nearer. Here the service was shorter and more vivid—there were frequent references to being washed in the blood of the Lamb. Sometimes I did not go to church at all on Sunday mornings. I was far from beginning to have doubts: I just felt that a disproportionate amount of my time had to be spent on churchgoing. However, when I went to Clacton to stay with my parents during the school holidays, although it was tacitly agreed that Sunday School days were over there was no escape from church twice on Sundays.

It was in the summer of 1933 at the height of the Silly Season that my father preached the sermon which was to affect his life if not the lives of his hearers for many years to come. On the 3rd September in that year in the course of his sermon, referring to entertainment being given on Sundays in Clacton Town Hall, he said:—

"I am appalled by the view of human nature which is held by those who are responsible for these programmes. They evidently are convinced that only an appeal to what is ignoble in man is likely to attract people. They are wrong, and do the greatest disservice to the good name of Clacton-on-Sea.

"I beg our visitors to believe that the Town Hall Sunday evening entertainments do not represent the mind of the town.

"They have been thrust upon us in ignorance.

"A crazy comedy night is offered as the attraction for a Sunday evening. I question whether there is another town or city in this country where the Municipal Buildings could be used for such a purpose. It is offensive in the extreme.

"I do not say there should be no Sunday entertainments. We are a free people, and I must respect the wishes of my fellows, though they differ from my own. But, when the Town Hall becomes responsible for such attractions as are offered by Clacton-on-Sea today the time for protest has come.

"I call upon the councillors, most of whom are men and women of sterling worth and who render great service to the town, to see that this scandal is not repeated another year. I also ask the Press, which is a credit to the country, to lend its great influence in this battle for a worthy Clacton-on-Sea.

"And, finally, I beg our churches both Established and Free to bear witness to the sacredness of the day by an unrelenting warfare against an evil which must alienate from our town all who seek wholesome enjoyment on their holidays and who resent and repudiate the imputation that their tastes are so depraved that nothing less than what is base can appeal to them, even on a Sunday.

"Let us see to it that our Town Hall does not become a Mecca for comedians whose vulgarity is a byword."

Although you might not think so from what I've told you so far my father was very far from being a strict Puritan in his outlook. He thoroughly enjoyed watching Everton and Liverpool, and was a film addict. In his youth he had frequented the Music Hall and saw Dan Leno often. He enjoyed a drink occasionally although my mother never drank, and he did not keep drink in the house. He smoked—he read, like many a bishop, hundreds of detective stories. He loved spending money on books, clothes and furniture. He drove his car as fast as it would go; fortunately he could not afford very big and powerful cars but he would have loved a Jag. He took us to concerts on the Pier at Clacton.

What on earth had been going on in the Town Hall to provoke this thunder clap? Strip shows, nudity, sexual perversions demonstrated live? No—you must make allowance for the fact that although in some other directions we may not have got very far, in mattters such as these we have progressed rapidly since 1933.

The Town Hall contained a theatre which was licensed for sacred Sunday concerts and visitors to Clacton had complained to my father about the entertainment which was offered them.

He preached his sermon; a reporter, Mr. Norman Harrison, who was a member of his church obtained a copy of his words and sent them to London. Next day there were headlines in the Evening Standard and other papers:

MINISTER ATTACKS TOWN HALL SUNDAY
ENTERTAINMENT DESIGNED TO APPEAL
TO ONLY THE BASE IGNOBLE AND
DEPRAVED TASTES

A few weeks later he was served with a writ, as were Mr. Harrison and the Evening Standard. A newspaper was worth suing even if Mr. Harrison and my father were not. The action came on for hearing in March 1935 before Mr. Justice Avory. Norman Birkett K.C. was the leader for my father—the junior was Brett Cloutman, V.C., M.C., who had been a friend of my father's since Muswell Hill days. Richard O'Sullivan K.C. was for the Plaintiffs and Roland Oliver K.C. appeared for Mr. Harrison and the Evening Standard. At the time Birkett was at the height of his fame and in his little leisure was a Methodist lay preacher. My father was entirely on his own and received no backing or support from the Baptist Union whatsoever until the trial was over.

Fourteen years later I met Birkett and asked him if he recalled the case. He was then a judge and had recently returned from the horror of the Nuremberg Trials. Quite a lot had happened in those fourteen years. He not only recalled the case but repeated to me on the spot a large chunk of his cross examination of one of the witnesses. A few days later he sent me a copy of an article from the Economist of the 16th March 1935 with a letter saying "apart from its humour it is a very fine vindication of your father." This is what the Economist said:—

"Mr. Hope, Mr. Palmer, Mrs. Argent, Mr. Williams, Mr. Hayden, Mr. Rennie, Mr. Page, Mr. Thomas, Mr. Sayer. What names are these? They are the names of nine people who have to their joint credit an achievement believed until this week to be all but impossible. Being plaintiffs in an action for libel and slander, they have in an English Court—before a special jury, in the year 1935, managed to lose their case. And what a loss it was! In the libel action the defendant was a great London evening paper, with plenty of money to tempt a jury into swingeing damages, and in the slander action he was a Baptist pastor round whom there doubtless hung that suspicion of radical views almost inseparable from his profession, and a taint of puritanism exactly calculated to inflame those manly prejudices that go with an old school tie and a special jury. And yet the defendants won.

"To understand this extraordinary case one must realise the simple fact that the authorities at Clacton-on-Sea, while providing their visitors with healthy amusement, are anxious to avoid even the appearance of vulgarity on all days of the week; but are so particularly anxious for Sundays that they have restricted the licence at the Town Hall on that day to sacred entertainment. In pursuit of this policy it was arranged that on one Sunday in 1934 the visitors should enjoy a sacred 'crazy comedy night', at which several of the plaintiffs in this action appeared. The Baptist minister, detecting from his old-fashioned puritanical standpoint a logical hiatus between the sacred licence and the crazy comedy, protested from the pulpit against the nature of the entertainment, and within a day or two was served with a writ by the indignant comedians and other artistes on the bill.

"The plaintiffs in one way were dreadfully unlucky. They found, when they came into court, that Mr. Norman Birkett, who appeared for the Baptist minister, had, so they complained, a gift which is, above all others, shocking to a music-hall comedian; the gift of bringing out a *double entendre* and making quite nice things sound quite nasty. Witnesses were frankly distressed at the meaning he could extract in court from simple lyrics which in their proper setting seem to have been practically spirituals. Take, for example, the little gem of a song that was sung on the Sunday in question by one of the plaintiffs, Mr. Thomas (billed as Mrs. Thomas' favourite husband), which told of an actress who was wearing tights. And they split. And she asked the audience for a pin. And someone was nearly killed in the crush. Hear that in the Sabbath calm of Clacton-on-Sea put over by Mr. Thomas, canonically dressed in 'a cap, a fifty-shilling suit and outsize brown boots,' and you could not, so it appears, either doubt the moral uplift or mistake the true note of the evangel. But the greatest things in art are like the rarest wines. Move them from their natural home and the bouquet passes. And it was sadly admitted by some of the witnesses that in court, on the less spiritual lips of Mr. Birkett, the spell was broken, the keen translunar music faded and the songs sounded not vulgar exactly, but what seems to be known in these sacred-entertainment circles as 'a bit on the blue side'.

"It is tempting at this point to give rein to one's imagination and speculate on the discussion that may have taken place when the authorities (whoever they are) who arrange the sacred menu for Clacton-on-Sea Sunday evenings met to discuss this particular programme. We can see the chairman (whoever he was) reminding his fellow-censors of the necessity to maintain undefiled the sacred character of what was to be offered to the audience. 'Of the first item on the programme, gentlemen (he would say), I have no doubt, and I submit it to you rather as a matter of form than for your serious consideration. It is a song called 'When are you going to lead me to the altar, Walter?' Nothing could fit more perfectly into the scheme of a sacred concert than this. It is a song in praise of the holy estate of matrimony, put into the mouth of a young girl who tells her bridegroom that, to her, marriage is so sacred that she will be content with no secular ceremony in a registry office, but insists upon the blessing of the Church, without which she could not look upon their union as the true and beautiful thing that it ought to be. You agree, gentlemen? Thank you. I pass over the suggested prizes for ladies in the audience wearing odd garters and flannel petticoats and for men with holes in their socks, because they are, I think, better suited to one of our week-day entertainments than to Sunday night. But the other song I have put before you, which treats of a singer whose tights split on the stage, conveys so strong a warning against the dangers of a fast life that it would, in my opinion, be a pity to remove it from the sacred into the secular programme. You agree? Thank you. That concludes the business of the meeting.'

"Really, when one comes to think of it, it ceases to be surprising even today that the comedians from Clacton-on-Sea lost their action. But it would be interesting to know why they even brought it. They were, no doubt, competently advised, and their advisers presumably knew what sort of turns they had been giving that Sunday night and the kind of dirt that counsel would have to whitewash when they came to argue the case to the jury. Probably the plaintiffs knew so much of what goes on now-a-days in the courts that they thought libel actions are a Tom Tiddler's ground on which anyone, unless he offends the special prejudices of a special jury, can pick up handfuls of money. They may have heard that such actions are, in the words of Lord Justice Maugham, profitable gold-digging operations, and believed that any case, however ludicrous, however flagrantly a waste of the court's time, however gross an imposition on a public-spirited critic performing a public duty, is nevertheless worth while as a try-on."

At the end of my father's evidence the judge bowed to him and in his summing up Mr. Justice Avory said:—

"Having seen Mr. Morris in the witness box it is for you to say whether you have ever seen a witness who was more obviously honest and straightforward. Have you ever seen a man who more honestly believed that he was doing his sacred duty in making that comment upon the services on Sunday evenings which really could only be held if they could properly be described as sacred? Can you doubt that Mr. Morris honestly believed that what was being done at the Town Hall was a grave violation not only of the terms of the licence but of all that was right and proper for Sunday concerts to which young girls might be taken in the belief that they were going to listen to a sacred performance?"

The case gave rise to considerable comment in the Press. The Spectator thought the verdict "a matter for profound satisfaction. It was a right and courageous use of the pulpit, abundantly vindicated in the result. It would be a disaster if fear of the law of libel checked just denunciations of social evils, and the growing laxity of the stage—not, of course, by any means the whole of it—has been carried to a point at which plain words about it are badly needed."

Not unnaturally the Evening Standard was also pleased and said that the verdict was "a vindication of a minister who spoke from his pulpit according to his conscience, and who faced protracted legal proceedings with calmness and courage."

The Times in a leader entitled "Sacred Concerts" wrote:—

"A wider world than Clacton-on-Sea, its inhabitants and visitors, has an interest in the libel and slander case concluded yesterday in the King's Bench. The case raised two important points—the abuse of a licence for sacred concerts on Sunday evenings and the question whether a church service is a 'meeting' within the meaning of the Act, which would allow a defence of 'fair report' to the charge. Mr. Justice Avory ruled that the service was such a public meeting. It remained for the jury to decide whether the Baptist minister's sermon, criticising the Sunday concerts at Clacton as being vulgar and worse, and the newspaper's report of the sermon were fair comment on a matter of public interest and without malice. The jury returned the obvious verdict and the Judge awarded costs against the plaintiffs, who were theatrical producers and artists concerned in the objectionable entertainments. No doubt was left by the evidence that some of what was offered as humour at these concerts was in the worst possible taste. The Judge described it a 'vulgarity and filth which took place deliberately in order to raise a laugh.' This was the kind of entertainment advertised as a sacred concert and attended, no doubt, by some persons who honestly believed that the performances advertised for Sunday evenings would come up to that description. It cannot be supposed, however, that the Town Council of Clacton, which let its Town Hall on Sundays for these performances and licensed them, was ignorant of their character. If the council could be supposed to be so ignorant it must have neglected its duty. But, in fact, one member of the Council, a turf accountant and chairman of the Entertainments Committee, stated in evidence that he attended the performances on every Sunday for two years and saw nothing objectionable in them. He must have had an exceptionally keen eye for an 'outsider' if he spotted anything sacred in them, though he expressed the opinion that nothing done by the artists was unfit for a sacred concert. The fact is, as admitted on behalf of the police, that the terms of the licence were habitually violated and that nobody in authority troubled about it until this minister made his protest. There may be more than one opinion as to the limits of what is permissible as humour in a public entertainment—they were certainly over-stepped at Clacton—and as to what is a suitable entertainment for Sundays. What is intolerable is that grossly vulgar entertainment should be licensed and presented as sacred."

A long article in The Tablet referred to his having "pluckily waged and won a perilous fight in the High Court of Justice." It concluded by saying:—

"We hope that Catholics, who have been so fully instructed and earnestly exhorted by their Holy Father and their Bishop to defend Christian modesty, will not fail to do all over the country what has been so manfully done by a brave Baptist at Clacton-on-Sea."

The Children's Newspaper congratulated Mr. Morris "for

his great service to a popular holiday town". "Those families," it said, "who take their holidays at Clacton-on-Sea will be thankful to Mr. Justice Avory and to the Baptist Minister of Clacton for the discouragement they have given to unhealthy Sunday entertainment there."

After the case my father received about a thousand letters of congratulation and support, many of them containing resolutions passed by various bodies up and down the country. Many came from Clergymen of other denominations, Anglican, Free Church and Roman Catholic. Several people who went out of their way to emphasise that they never went to church also wrote with favourable comments, including one gentleman who sent a cheque with the explanation that though he drank like a fish and carried on with women he did believe in the sanctity of the English Sabbath.

It is clear from the comments in the correspondence and the press that the main support for my father's stand came from two different groups which did not necessarily coincide. One group was particularly concerned to protect the traditional English Sunday, the other was more concerned about standards of morality generally on the stage. What either group would have thought of the present situation seems fairly clear, but whether there would be a similar volume of support for such a stand today seems doubtful. Perhaps some prominent church figure would care to preach a similar sermon to test public reaction?

But there is a difficulty in seeking to join the issue of protecting the English Sunday with general standards of morality in public performances. In his sermon which caused all the trouble my father referred to those "who resent and repudiate the imputation that their tastes are so depraved that nothing less than what is base can appeal to them, *even on a Sunday.*" (my italics.)

In a sermon he preached in March 1935, after the verdict he is reported as having said:—

"I know that the pendulum has swung to the other

extreme, and that the puritanism of our fathers is no longer acceptable to people. The only church which can possibly appeal to people is the church salted with laughter and joy, but, nevertheless, when you have made allowance for these things, you and I are convinced today of this significant fact: That in the leisure hours of people, in their amusements, they may be subjected to vulgarity, which, in the words of the judge himself, was 'nothing less than filth'.

"I say the church must insist that on the one hand is darkness, and on the other is light, and light is Christ."

The report continued:—

Proceeding, Mr Morris said the case further established that the Christian Sabbath was still one of the moral foundations of the British people. He asked them to note that what was wrong on a week-day was wrong on a Sunday, and that a thing that was right on Sunday was also right on a week-day. They could not make a distinction, but nevertheless, there was a distinct feeling in the court that Sunday was a day set apart, a day which had been consecrated by the history of good men and women, who had embodied therein the idealism and faith of the British people, and that it would be a bad time when that distinction between week-day and Sunday was permitted to disappear. There was something peculiar in the Sabbath.

"Did they, as Christian men and women, make the witness they should of the sanctity of the Sabbath? Did they, by unswerving fidelity to these principles of the Sabbath, make it possible for the day to remain part of the glorious heritage of the people?

"Since the case, he had received many letters from all kinds of people, some of them unbelievers and agnostics, but they all insisted that the Sabbath should be kept clean and sweet, in the most real sense holden to God. It was their first responsibility to maintain the Sabbath. He remembered that Israel fell when the Sabbath lost its spiritual sanctity, and he believed that modern democracy was dying because it lacked the spiritual dynamic."

E

"What was wrong on a week-day was wrong on a Sunday, and that a thing that was right on Sunday was also right on a week-day. They could not make a distinction"—but nevertheless he went on to attempt to make one. The same attempt was made by Sir John Foster Fraser in an article entitled "The Vulgarity Business" in the Sunday Graphic and Sunday News. Writing in the issue of the 17th March 1935 he said:—

"Now we can consider different brands of British humour: clean, broad, vulgar, and even that which depends on filth to raise a laugh.

"And most of us commend the Rev. Samuel Mordecai Morris, minister of the Baptist Church at Clacton-on-Sea, for being outspoken in his pulpit and standing up to a charge of slander in the High Court of Justice—and winning his case.

"I don't know if Mr. Morris is a strict Sabbatarian within the customary meaning, and thinks we should all spend the Sabbath in church ruminating on what will happen if we do not cease being miserable sinners.

"I would like to believe he is one of those parsons who believe in a joyful Sunday, and that to be healthfully happy is not yielding to the cunning devices of Old Nick.

"Anyway, he has courageously protested against the degredation of the Sunday—not that what is objectionable on Sunday should receive approval on Saturday or any other evening of the week."

*   *   *

"We have two groups of thought: one that the English Sunday is dreary, Puritanic, long-faced, all pleasure scowled upon, and that for the ordinary man there is little to do but yawn through hours of boredom and go to bed at nine o'clock —which is not true; and one that it is 'Continental,' entirely losing its significance, religion ignored and devoted to revelry and unseemly pleasure—and that is not true either.

"There is a pleasant mean between chilly Calvinism and

roystering Rabelaisianism. That is where I like to relax . . .

"We British are prone to put our hands on our chests and give thanks to heaven for all the national virtues we possess.

"We are hypocritical though we bluff ourselves with smugness. Popular taste is not high. The snigger is more general than the hearty laugh. But while most of us want to get away from the bleak and depressing Sabbatarianism we do not want Sunday to degenerate into a special occasion for unwholesome pleasures . . .

"Reverence for Sunday is in the bones of most of us. I've a sort of satisfaction that not much of the theological savagery of my Presbyterian forbears remains with me; but there is a deep-down love for the beauty of Sunday which I could not get rid of if I tried. There is a special aroma about Sunday, a peace, a restfulness, a hallowedness which cannot be explained but can be felt.

"Elder readers may recall some of the blackness of the old Sunday when our fathers put on their 'blacks' to go to kirk, and it was evidence of piety to pull down the front room blinds on the Sabbath, as though a peep of sunshine on the hillside was not quite in consonance with the tenor of the day. You've heard the story of the English visitor to Skye. 'It's a fine day,' said he. 'This is no' the day to be talking about fine days,' said the man of Skye."

What would either the strict Sabbatarians or the upholders of stage morality standards say now?

"In the revolt against the restraints and proprieties of the Victorian world, the pendulum has swung to the other extreme. Music has gone back to the African jungle for its inspiration. Art has rebelled against beauty. Religion is abandoned as an old wives' tale and sex has become the chief preoccupation of literature . . . It is not enough to have released women from the bondage and absurdities of Victorian dress: we must, as a recent writer in the New Statesman did, exalt nudity as a new and inspiring religion that is to wash us clean of all our spiritual ailments. It is not enough to have got more frank and sensible relations between the sexes: we must talk about nothing but sex . . . There is money in indecency and there are always harpies ready to exploit it. And it is being exploited today on the stage and in literature with a flagrant and unblushing impudence that would have shocked even the England of the Restoration. Hardly a play appears without its bedroom scene and half the films that are shown have cuckoldry for their theme. Eminent authors describe scenes of a seduction with a particularity that, if it were employed at their table by a visitor, would lead to him being handed his hat and coat and shown to the door . . .''

Those words seem to sum up the feelings of many towards today's permissive society. They come from an article entitled "We Don't Want these Nasty New Morals" by A. L. Gardiner in John Bull of the 23rd March 1935, an article hung on the peg of the Clacton libel case.

Amongst the many letters which my father received he was especially pleased to hear from Spurgeon's College and the following letter from a Congregational Minister must have given him great pleasure:—

March 14th., 35.

Dear Mr. Morris,

One hesitates to add to what must be a sufficiently full mail—and I seldom write to men I don't happen to know— but I should feel personal loss if I didn't join in the chorus of thanks and congratulation.

You have done the ministry a real good turn, and it is a thrilling thing to read the Judge's tribute to your demeanour in the box. And now that the tumult is over you are sure to be feeling the strain—so may I assure you of my prayers and good wishes.

Once when I was holidaying at my old home in Liverpool I dropped in at Myrtle Street—in July 1931. If ever our paths cross I must ask for the MSS of that sermon; it moved me so much that I wrote about the experience in my magazine—a thing I have never done before or since. I always think of it as one of the greatest things I ever heard. Evening of July 19th, 1931.

I don't know how the money side of this business is going to pan out, but if there is need you ought to give other folk than your own a chance of standing in.

With all good wishes,
Yours sincerely,
R. G. Parry.

It is a considerable tribute to his preaching abilities from a fellow preacher, and in the years following the libel case there were often half a dozen or more Free Church Ministers in the congregation at Clacton on a summer evening listening to my father preach. Sometimes when they sat near my mother and me I would hear them at the end of the service saying what a wonderful sermon it had been and I felt a surge of pride.

This letter, as did many others, also offered financial help. Although my father was awarded the costs of the action there was a difference of £500 between what he had to pay his own lawyer and what was recoverable from the losers. The money was soon raised by contributions from all over the country. Unfortunately some years later the Plaintiffs could not pay all the costs which were due from them and once again a considerable burden of anxiety was placed on my father. It was only shortly before the war that with generous help the costs question was finally cleared up. From the time when he first preached his sermon until the costs were finally paid was a period of about six years. He aged far more than six years during that period.

Gradually the letters ceased to flow, the invitations to address public meetings slowed down, the nine day wonder was over. England resumed its dreamwalk to 1939. People were more interested in the Rector of Stiffkey than the Baptist Minister of Clacton.

Spurgeon himself was also concerned with Sunday concerts. Before the Tabernacle was built and at a time when he was already attracting vast audiences he began holding services in the Surrey Music Hall which was capable of holding about ten thousand people. His biographer W. Y. Fullerton writes:—

"It was erected in the Royal Surrey Gardens for concert purposes, and the bold idea occurred to several people that it might be utilised for Mr. Spurgeon's services. Some thought it would be too large, others that it would be very unsuitable to hold Divine service in a place of worldly amusement."

The first service was held on a Sunday evening on the 19th October 1856 with ten thousand people inside and another ten thousand outside in the gardens—for three years Spurgeon preached at a morning service at the Music Hall.

"To gain entrance to the services, tickets were necessary . . . a service in 1857 is described by an 'eye witness': 'Every seat was occupied by half past ten o'clock, when the doors were opened to the public, then there was a rush of excited and hurried people, and in ten minutes every inch of standing room was occupied. Dr. Livingstone sat on the platform, and the Princess Royal, as well as the Duchess of Sutherland, were said to be present.' "

Spurgeon's association with the Sunday Music Hall ended because he learnt that the proprietors were proposing to allow the Hall to be used on Sunday Evenings for concerts. No doubt only the staidest performances were intended, perhaps only sacred performances were allowed; probably the words "Music Hall" did not then connote those reputedly marvellous haunts of varied talents of the pre-1914 era. However, "The Sunday concerts did not prosper, the income from the Sunday services was lost, and in trying to make the best of both worlds (the proprietors) gained neither, becoming bankrupt soon afterwards."

In the light of Spurgeon's and my father's experience should one trace a Divine connection between Sunday concerts and bankruptcy?

My father himself was feeling the financial strain. His

income was considerably less than at Liverpool, and his ambition for me was costing him, even taking into account a scholarship, nearly a quarter of his income. In the thirties we had only one holiday of five days and my mother supplemented the family budget by taking in paying visitors during the summer season. My father always tended to overspend whilst she had the anxiety of saving and being careful. Assuming that I would follow his habits, his first step when I opened a bank account of my own was to tell the Bank Manager he would guarantee a small overdraft. But although our material standards were declining, we were still far better off than most people—certainly than my unemployed miner uncle and his family in Morriston, and a visit there soon taught me the realities of life.

Throughout the teens, which I spent at boarding school, I loved the holidays at Clacton. Moments and hours of marvellous communion with my father were interspersed with hellish rows. We both always knew the other's mood and thoughts—a rather dangerous state of affairs. In any crisis I knew he would be behind me like the Rock of Ages only more comforting. The minor irritations and irritabilities of every day life would be forgotten. I bet a friend that I could fire my airgun against the palm of my hand without suffering any harm. I pulled the trigger and lost my bet. My father didn't say what a bloody fool I'd been. He was interested and sympathetic and gentle over my religious doubts. Even after a row when I hated him I still found his preaching spellbinding. Even though I knew his little characteristics, his gestures, the format of his sermons—time after time the fire of his faith and the energy of his eloquence would carry me away and we would enjoy the wonderful haven of peace on the Sunday evening together—reading or talking quietly. He was always ready to listen and willing to talk and he never pretended there were no difficulties. He began to preach pacifist sermons and A. A. Milne, Dick Shepard and Beverley Nicholls began to influence my thoughts.

By the age of about seventeen I began to wonder whether I should be baptised.

The Baptists now number over thirty million throughout the world and their churches stretch from the deep south of America to Soviet Russia. The main characteristic which distinguishes them from other denominations, apart from their system of self-government, is that they practise Believers' Baptism, that is, they believe that one should witness to one's acceptance of Christianity by a symbolic act and at an age of discretion. The symbolic act is now and has been for some time immersion in water; a practice which was common throughout the church during the first centuries and is still provided for in the Book of Common Prayer.

Then the Priest shall take the child into his hands and shall say to the Godfathers and Godmothers,

Name this Child

And then naming it after them (if they shall certify him that the child may well endure it) he shall dip it in the water, discreetly and warily, saying

I baptise thee in the name of the Father, and of the Son, and of the Holy Ghost. Amen.

But if they certify that the child is weak, it shall suffice to pour water upon it, saying the foresaid words.

The Prayer Book also provides that infant Baptism should usually take place during the service of Morning or Evening Prayer—a practice which is universally ignored. Nowadays Anglicans practise infant baptism by a sprinkling of water. Curiously enough so did the first Baptists, but now they practise immersion.

Scattered up and down the country in hundreds of ugly chapels there are a series of large baths or small swimming pools usually hidden, by floor boards, when not in use. Before one can be baptised one has to be visited by deacons of the church who ask questions to test one's religious sincerity. I think that in my case, as the Minister's son, I was given favourable treatment and the benefit of any doubt. The questions were few and I was passed spiritually fit for baptism. On the day, usually at the end of the evening service and in the presence of the whole congregation, the decks having been cleared for action and the bath filled with water the Minister climbs down into the pool clothed in black waterproof clothes while those about to be baptised wait at one side. As the congregation sings hymns, one by one they enter the water. My turn came and with the words spoken, softly, "relax and rely on me", and, loudly, "David Elwyn, I baptise thee in the name of the Father and of the Son and of the Holy Ghost", my father whipped me over backwards and ducked me in the pool.

I was certainly not so presumptuous as to expect the heavens to open, but I was very keyed up and a little disappointed not to feel any different on emerging from the pool from what I had felt on entering it—although considerably wetter. However, the ceremony over I was entitled to become a full member of the church.

I could attend church meetings, take part in the discussion of church business, vote for the election of Deacons, even voice my views in the choice of a new Minister. I could also take part in the Communion Service and if I felt no especial religious experience at my baptism I never failed to feel a sense of religious awe during the Communion Service. In my early teens when I had been staying with some schoolfriends in an Anglican family I had been taken to the local parish church one Sunday. It was a Communion Service. At the appropriate moment the family left their pews, walked up to the priest at the altar, knelt and received the wine from the cup. The others seemed to take it for granted that I should go too and so, frightened of making a fuss or seeming different, I also went, knelt and took the wine. I still remember the sight and feel of the cup. I hope I did not do wrong. But it was all very strange to me.

E*

In the Baptist Church the Communion Service is usually held once a month at the end of the Evening Service. A table is set at the front of the congregation. On it are plates of bread cubes and stands containing very small tumblers of wine. As at the Last Supper the Minister sits at the table surrounded by his Deacons, who might be a shopkeeper or two, an engine driver, a tailor, a nursery man or a doctor. The Minister serves his Deacons with bread and wine. The Deacons then serve the congregation with bread and wine. Then, as the Minister repeats those amazing words, Minister, Deacons and congregation, facing one another, eat the bread simultaneously and then drink the wine simultaneously. The wonderful beauty of the service, the charged atmosphere is slightly spoilt by the noise made when the small glass tumblers are put down on the shelves of the wooden pews in a tiny, pattering, fusillade. In the Baptist service all eat and drink together at the same time in the body of the church. In the Anglican service the priest takes the Communion alone and apart. In the Baptist Service each drinks from a separate tumbler, in the Anglican Service all drink the wine from the same cup. Most Baptist Churches welcome to Communion anyone who professes to believe in and follow Jesus Christ. The Anglican Service is theoretically at least not open to those who have not been confirmed as members of the Church of England. The Anglican Service is ambiguous.

"Grant us therefore, gracious Lord, so to eat the flesh of thy dear Son Jesus Christ, and to drink his blood, that our sinful bodies may be made clean by his body, and our souls washed through his most precious blood . . ."
Article XXVIII
". . . the Bread which we break is a partaking of the Body of Christ, and likewise the Cup of Blessing is a partaking of the Blood of Christ . . ."
but later
"The Body of Christ is given, taken, and eaten in the Supper, only after a heavenly and spiritual manner . . ."

The uneasy ghost of transubstantiation does not lurk in the simpler, Baptist service.

Before any real test could be carried out of my value in my new role as a Church Member there came the outbreak of the Second World War. For the first and only time in my life I saw my father weeping. My feelings were rather those of relief. The long agony of waiting for Hitler was over.

For a few months of phoney war Clacton-on-Sea continued almost normally—deserted and quiet—but then it always was deserted and quiet in the winter. Then came the shattering blows of 1940 and most of the population of Clacton as in other coastal towns was evacuated. Writing at the time I noted:—

"Tomorrow we leave for London. My father stays behind as a Minister of Religion. I take my mother to London by car. In Clacton there are guns all along the coast, barbed wire all along the shore, search lights, A.A. guns, Bren guns, gun emplacements, sand-bags everywhere. There must be several thousands of soldiers in the town including some of the B.E.F. just back from France, and some of the New Zealanders. Some expect an invasion any moment. Some think that it will not occur for months if at all."

We went to London where my mother went to live at her father's home—her mother had died of cancer soon after her golden wedding just before the War.

The evacuation of Clacton save for a few civilians meant the end, at least "for the duration", of my father's church. The death of Myrtle Street had been postponed for a few years after his departure. The church at Clacton died under him. He had no income at all and he was fifty two years old. He lived in our old house, now almost empty of furniture, by himself. He ministered to the troops, many of whom were being frozen in one of Mr. Butlin's Holiday Camps which had not been designed for winter occupation. He travelled up and down between London and Clacton on a moped. My mother went back to work in a Bank where she had worked before marrying in the First World War. My father became an insurance salesman. As he soon came to believe as passionately in the value of insurance as he did in the doctrine of Christianity and as he brought to selling policies all the vigour of his preaching and his Welsh charm, his persuasive efforts were so successful that he was soon considerably more prosperous as an insurance salesman that he had ever been as a Baptist Minister. I still have a silver cigarette box awarded to him by his Company for having sold some colossal sum of insurance policies in one month.

Guide me, O Thou Great Jehovah,
Pilgrim through this barren land;
I am weak, but Thou are mighty;
Hold me with Thy powerful hand:
  Bread of heaven,
Feed me now and evermore.

Open now the crystal fountain,
Whence the healing stream doth flow;
Let the fiery cloudy pillar
Lead me all my journey through:
  Strong Deliverer,
Be Thou still my strength and shield.

When I tread the verge of Jordan,
Bid my anxious fears subside;
Death of death, and hell's Destruction,
Land me safe on Canaan's side.
  Songs of praises
I will ever give to Thee.

WILLIAM WILLIAMS OF PANTYCELYN (1716–91)

Five

A whisper in an empty church
at Oswaldtwistle

In the Twenties the Welsh National Eisteddfod was held in Liverpool and my father took me along to hear Lloyd George speak. As he spoke in Welsh I could not understand a word he said, but I remember the volume of applause that greeted his arrival on the platform. He could have had no more fervent admirer than my father—a fellow Welshman, a fellow Baptist, the man who had broken the power of the English landed aristocracy, the man who had won the war, he symbolised in his person the link between non-conformity and liberalism. My father was not to know that Ll. G. also contained within him the symbol of the decay of both; that his private life showed considerable departures from his Puritan upbringing, that the split with Asquith had fatally weakened the party before the advance of Labour, that this arch-enemy of the landed aristocracy who won the First World War would die as an Earl in the Second World War doubting a British victory.

The writing was already on the wall by the Twenties but I don't think my father saw it. He voted Liberal as he had always done. "After 1880", says R. C. K. Ensor "they (the Liberals) had paid increasing attention to the lower sections of the middle class and the upper strata of the wage earners; and since these were mainly non-conformist, had enrolled non-conformity. By so doing they revived the historic tie between the Tory party and the established church . . . The more the Liberals came to rely on the chapels, the more public houses rallied to their opponents."

As a result of the Liberal non-conformist alliance Oxford and Cambridge Universities were opened to dissenters and Parnell's fate was sealed. Immediately after Captain O'Shea obtained a decree nisi against his wife on the 17th November 1890 the National Liberal Federation met at Sheffield and it was "privately represented to the Front Bench in the persons of Morley and Harcourt that English non-conformists could not continue any association with the Irish party unless it changed its leader. This line was quite a sincere and natural one for religious Victorians to take. The persons chiefly responsible for focusing opinion upon it were the Rev. Hugh Price Hughes, one of the most influential ministers in the Wesleyan connexion; W. T. Stead in the Review of Reviews; and E. T. Cook, in the Pall Mall Gazette."

The alliance between Liberals and non-conformity reached its peak in the famous parliament of 1906 when the Liberals were returned with a majority of eighty four over all other parties. A hundred years earlier a group of non-conformist merchants had decided to establish a boarding school for their sons and they eventually agreed to buy "a very commodious house at Mill Hill, Hendon, a situation peculiarly pleasant and salubrious, where they hoped many of the rising generation would imbibe the elements of sound literature and the principles of Evangelical religion, and thus become a credit to the institution, the joy of their parents, and blessings in every relation of social life." At the centenary celebration in 1907 the Prime Minister Sir Henry Campbell-Bannerman made a speech and there were seven former members of the school who were M.P.s on the platform.

By the thirties another man who was the son of a non-conformist minister and who had been educated at Mill Hill School was proving to be one of the most brilliant propagandists any political party has ever had; but Kingsley Martin was serving the Labour and not the Liberal cause.

In Wales the links between the Liberal Party and non-conformity had been even stronger than in England. The authors of "Social Change in South West Wales", writing of the Swansea area, have said that in the nineteenth century it was a Liberal stronghold. "The strength of the Liberal vote, too, reflected the major division in local society—church and chapel. In the generation before the First World War there were few differences between the chapels and the Liberal Party either in personnel or policies, and it was not uncommon for the chapels to act as Liberal platforms. A main cause of this unity may have been the drive for the disestablishment of the church, which was connected also with a growing nationalism. Liberalism in politics reflected the radical element in Welsh life . . ."

And again they say

"Before the First World War there was a serious division in Welsh society; Anglican religion, Conservatism, landowners and industrialists on the one side; Nonconformity, Liberalism, farmers, lower middle class, and working class on the other. The culmination of the conflicts based on this division came with the disestablishment of the Church of England in Wales by the Act of 1914.

"Since the conclusion of the Disestablishment Campaign, the churches have retired from the field of political controversy, or it might be truer to say that they have not extended their interest in social questions in a way which would have kept them in that field. The causes for which the Non-conformist Liberals mainly fought have long since been successful: disestablishment, educational reform, the reform of tithes and church rates, the right of Non-conformist ministers to perform the burial service, and so forth."

What had once been a Liberal stronghold fell to Labour, and although some Non-conformist ministers became Labour supporters the link between Non-conformity and Labour has never been as strong as that between Non-conformity and the Liberal Party at its zenith. The authors of "Social Change in South West Wales" say that the conclusion they have come to is that "in the 1920s and 1930s working people began to withdraw from the chapels . . . chapels were becoming less attractive than they had been to active trade unionists and Labour Party people because they were not facing up to the realities of the class struggle as they appeared to the local working class."

Meanwhile, writing of the period between 1901–14, R. C. K. Ensor says:—

"The chapels kept up their congregations better than the Church of England; but the Labour and Socialist movement poached extensively on their preserves. Not only . . . did it provide careers on the platform for gifted men who would otherwise have found them in the pulpit but the I.L.P., which made a practice of holding large indoor propaganda meetings on Sunday evenings, directly drew away the members of congregations. The ministers of the chapels, feeling the attraction which the new politics had for their people, very often went to meet it halfway. An institution which spread widely at this time was the 'P.S.A.' (Pleasant Sunday Afternoon); held as a rule in the chapel itself with the minister presiding, but, save for a short prayer and hymns, secular in character. Usually there were songs or other solo music, but the main feature was an address by a layman on a secular subject, oftenest with a bias to humanitarianism of some kind. Popular authors, travellers, politicians, journalists, or socialist propagandists were in great request for these addresses— especially the last; and it is significant of the political trend of non-conformity in these years, that while few Conservative politicians were invited to speak at P.S.A.S. and many Liberals were not either, a leading Socialist might spend practically every Sunday afternoon in them. The sects, however, differed somewhat in this respect, and the contacts of Socialism were common and closer with the Congregational and Baptist chapels than with the Wesleyan.

"One way and another the rising Labour movement owed an immense debt to non-conformity. The fund of unselfish idealism, which sustained the early I.L.P., came mostly from this source; and the methods whereby its branches were run and financed were borrowed directly by its members from their experience in religious organisations. Broadly it was due to non-conformity that Socialism in England never acquired the anti-religious bias prevailing on the Continent."

In the 1906 election the Liberals won 377 seats. 53 Labour members were returned. By 1922 Labour had 4,237,349 votes and 142 seats; the Liberals 4,080,915 and 115 seats. Two years later Labour had 151 seats and the Liberals 40. By 1935 the Liberals were down to 21. Since the Second World War, although over 6 million have still voted Liberal as late as 1974, the party has been lucky to get double figures in seats.

In the 1945 election my father, who had always previously voted Liberal, voted Labour for the first time, and continued to vote Labour until he died.

Mention Oswaldtwistle to a southerner. At first he will smile as he mentally classifies it together with Wigan Pier as a Music Hall joke, a place of myth, a symbol of all that is ludicrous about Lancashire. The smile will be followed by a look of genuine amazement when one insists that the place actually exists. It lies on the northernmost fringe of industrial Lancashire in a great hollow in the moors, merging with Accrington, row upon row of harsh grey streets, the townscape punctuated by the vertical exclamation marks of disused cotton mill chimneys. Although the sun must shine there sometimes, whenever I go it seems to be on days of dark clouds and sweeping rain so that the grey stones of the houses look almost black and shiny.

Isolated at one end of the town stand two churches, an Anglican church and a Baptist Chapel. It is the custom amongst Baptist Churches to hold special anniversary services once or twice a year at which visiting preachers are invited to conduct the proceedings and preach. My father had first been invited to preach at these services at New Lane Oswaldtwistle when he was at Liverpool and the invitation was repeated annually for years. Visiting preachers usually arrive on Saturday and leave on Monday and they are given hospitality by members of the church. My father was particularly lucky with his host at Oswaldtwistle and developed a warm friendship with Tom Pickup and his wife. The services were a great success, the chapel was packed full morning and evening and a collection of several hundred pounds was taken. After the evening service an enormous meal was eaten in the Pickups' home. I became friendly with their two sons to who I am indebted for teaching me to smoke.

Towards the end of the war my father had become minister of a church at Ipswich, but in 1951 he was invited to become minister at Oswaldtwistle which he had known for thirty years. By now he was sixty four years old and any move would almost certainly be the last one. Quite apart from his wish to go on preaching, he had to because through some quirk of the Welfare State he did not qualify for an old age pension until he was seventy. He hesitated—my mother was happier in the south. While he was still wondering what to do he received a letter from Rev. S. G. Morris, a well known and much loved Baptist Minister. It was dated 18th July 1951 and said:—

"Dear Namesake,
Whose name is lower on the list, but higher in other respects.
Thanks for generous sub which I have already handed over.
You need a rebuke! You *must* not talk about growing old and finishing up, and all that—
You go north again where you are known and loved—and your talents and experience fits you for the *leadership*—which, I am sure you will exercise—so put *that* in your pipe—if you still afford one . . .
Now be good S. M. and do as I tell you,
My love to you both,

Affectionately yours,
S. G.

My father took the advice and moved in the autumn. In a way he was going home—not back to Wales and Morriston but to somewhere very like it—to an industrial village or small town where one feels that the basic realities of life show through and neighbours share one another's burdens. Mills were closing, chimneys gave out no smoke, there were many to remember the grim thirties, many whose whole lives were wrapped up with the decline of what had once been the greatest cotton industry in the world. Now cloth caps were still to be seen but not universely—clogs and shawls were almost gone. Patches of new council houses surrounded the old grey streets, smart young women pushed posh looking prams. In some roads cars were parked outside houses.

The Baptist Chapel was a grey stone building, approached through a small graveyard whose headstones were of an even darker grey. A few steps led up to a small vestibule from which two doors led into the body of the chapel, consisting of two aisles and three blocks of pitch pine pews whose varnish was sticky enough to remove tufts from trousers if pressed too hard against the next pew. The pulpit was central and high. Still higher and behind sat the choir, and highest of all was the organist, the pipes of whose organ formed a symetrical pattern to the roof of tubes great and small. On each side of the pulpit two more doors led into vestries and rooms where the choir assembled. Inside the church a gallery surrounded three sides of the building, supported on slender, decorated metal shafts. The windows were of plain glass and the walls plastered. In front of the pulpit, covered when not in use, was the baptistry. The building was capable of seating seven to eight hundred people. It was a building whose main features have been repeated in countless Free Churches up and down the country. It was simple, functional and not without grace, its bareness as moving as the history washed stone of some old village church. It was a place in which to worship God, a place which proclaimed that the pulpit and the preacher were central to the service of worship.

For my father the last battle had begun. No longer was he the well known and popular visiting preacher from Liverpool inspiring and being inspired by a full church at an anniversary service. Sunday by Sunday the congregation numbered tens where he had known hundreds. Not far from the Baptist Chapel one evening Tom Pickup was knocked down and killed by a passing car. Within a year of moving from Ipswich my mother had died of cancer. Soon afterwards my father had an operation for the removal of the gall bladder with a fistful of stones, then prostate trouble, then months of slow consuming cancer.

As for his income which had gone down to three hundred and fifty a year and a manse at Ipswich, it was now even lower. For Hugh Stowell Brown it had been rather different.

" 'The world has a trick of setting itself right', said a farmer to me.

"After all the bad weather and eight months of winter, we are likely to have good crops, and the weather is glorious. Perhaps the saying will prove true of trade, in which I am myself a sufferer, having so far this year received from *one* source of income only £100 instead of £300 as usual."

So that the probability is that in investment income alone he had an income far in excess in real terms of what my father and many other Ministers of all denominations were struggling on by the mid Twentieth Century.

The following is from The Guardian of 23rd November 1970 under a headline "CLERGY BELOW POVERTY LINE":—

"Many Baptist ministers will still be living below the poverty line even when the proposed £60 a year rise is paid.

"Minimum earnings for a married minister will be just over £17 a week from next January. But, even after rentfree housing and small service and children's allowances, some will still be expected to apply for help under the Government's supplementary incomes system.

"The Government regards £18 as a minimum weekly earnings for a married man with one child. The Baptists' rate will be £18.07.

"Other comparisons include an official minimum of £20 a week for a married man with two children against the Baptists' £18.40, and £22 a week for three children against £18.65.

"A spokesman at the Baptist Union headquarters in London, said yesterday that the official poverty line confirmed how badly ministers' pay had been slipping behind those of other denominations and professions.

"A leading article in the current issue of the Baptist Times puts it more bluntly, saying that it is no disgrace for ministers to be reckoned among the poor. What is a disgrace is for fellow disciples to allow them to live below the poverty line.

"Some ministers will not even get the extra £60 because their local churches are too independent to ask the union for help."

Other denominations are little better off.

In the autumn of 1957 I heard him preach for the last time. I had been travelling by road and had told him that I would be there for the evening service. I was late and the service had begun when I got to the church. I decided to go upstairs to the gallery—it was completely empty and downstairs there was a scattered, tiny congregation. As I sat down my father looked up and gave me the most marvellous smile of welcome.

Three months later the cancer had reached the vocal chords and he could only just speak in a whisper. He had to give up preaching but he only died slowly over a period of months.

"The days of our years are three score and ten; and if by reason of strength they may be fourscore years, yet is their strength, labour and sorrow; for it is soon cut off, and we fly away."

As he died by inches, year by year churches were closing.

According to The Times of the 24th February 1972:—

"There are 18,000 parish churches in England on which the Church of England spends over £13,000,000 annually for the maintenance of worship, yet the future of half of them is debatable and a third may disappear by the end of the century . . ."

Year by year the receding tide of Empire was leaving on our shores an increasing flotsam of other religions. Enoch Powell has summed it up thus:—

"I have before me a news picture, published a year or two ago in a local paper, which shows the then Rector of Wolverhampton (now Bishop of Shrewsbury) at a celebration of the Hindu Durga Puja in the town, which was attended by Hindus from all over the Midlands. The accompanying text informs us that an idol of Durga of great sanctity had been flown from Calcutta specially for the festival.

"The predicament of the rector in that temple-room in Wolverhampton typifies from one aspect the predicament of the Church as a whole in England today. That predicament has in no wise been created by the presence in England of large and increasing populations of Muslims and followers of other religions. Their presence has only served to sharpen its outlines.

"The Church is by nature and of necessity missionary, because it asserts its gospel both to be unique and indispensable and also to be addressed and available to all mankind. It is not, for instance, like Judaism, uniquely true but addressed to a particular race. It is not, like Hinduism, tolerant of all beliefs and none, but limited to the population of a certain sub-continent. Consequently, those who said the Creed and received the sacraments in English towns and villages were told and accepted, that they were obliged, so far as in them lay, to support and further the preaching of the gospel and the extension of the Church in 'heathen lands afar'.

"The first searching challenge did not, as it happened,

originate 'afar', it arose when a substantial, and presently a large, part of the population of England itself ceased to belong (other than nominally, if that) to any body professing the Christian faith. The question then was, 'With what conviction can we send missions to the heathen afar, when the heathen are here at home, our own kith and kin, in our own land? The mission field, surely, has come home?'

"At the same time as the mission field was folding up overseas, England was in the early stages of a revolutionary change in the composition of her population, to which there has been no precedent or parallel. The Christian Church, on which Asia and Africa were closing their doors as being the cultural badge of the west, was now confronted in England by the religious and cultural badges of large and growing communities transplanted from the very lands where, if 'thick darkness' brooded when the hymn was written, no less 'thick darkness broodeth yet'. Mosques, temples and gurudwaras not only arose round the churches, but actually displaced some of them and took over the buildings."

And Sikhs at Runnymede were doing their best to make a Ganges of the Thames.

By January 1971 we had progressed to the stage where on the same page of The Times it could be reported that:—

"A South London church, built in 1820 to celebrate the Battle of Waterloo, may be converted into seven luxury flats if plans are approved by Southwark Council . . . Mr. Richard Pollock, the architect responsible for the design of the flats, said: 'The exterior of the church, *the most important part of the building,* (my italics) will not be spoilt in any way. From the outside it will always look what it is, a fine classical church which everyone is anxious to preserve."

How splendid at the end of Conservation Year actually to plan for "whited sepulchres, which indeed appear beautiful outward, but are within full of dead men's bones . . ."

On the same page lower down the following appears:—

SEX SHOP ANGERS CLERGYMEN

"Mr. Henry Wood, a shopkeeper, has angered the local clergy by opening a sex supermarket next door to a church. The supermarket, which is called The Birds and Bees, is in Windsor Road, Slough, and sells stimulants, contraceptives and aphrodisiacs.

"The minister of the church, the Rev. William Clarke, who said the store was an indication of a sick society, has called a special meeting of his church executive to try to get it closed down. Mr. Wood says he will ignore the protests."

Writing of the mental and social aspects of English history between 1886 and 1890 R. C. K. Ensor has said:—

"Intellectual men were deterred from orders not merely or always (though after 1886 very commonly) by doctrinal doubt, but because they no longer felt that church-going was the most central of their concerns. Not only rival interests, but rival careers were fast developing—the new Civil Service, the new openings in education and research, the higher journalism, and a variety of business callings, some (like electrical engineering) quite new, and others which, though old, had (like the solicitor's profession) greatly expanded in public esteem and social standing.

"Non-conformity, in its own sphere, receded much less during these years; but it too suffered in its recruitment of ministers from a worldly competition. Down to the eighties a gifted boy in the humblest classes found his only obvious escape in the chapels; if he possessed any talent for oratory he would become a preacher, and in that way reach the goal of black-coated professional status. But from 1884 onwards a rival 'escape' appeared in the Labour movement. In the eighties and nineties a great many men became trade-union officials or socialist agitators (with a cabinet minister's seals of office in their knapsacks), who, had they been born twenty years earlier, would have made careers like Spurgeon's or General Booth's. To say this is not to impugn their sincerity in either case, but to recognise that human ability, like water, will rise to its level through the directest channel that may be open at any given time. The effects were of course not immediately felt; but in many great working-class areas (e.g. the South Wales coal field) they showed themselves very markedly during the first quarter of the present century."

I doubt whether my father had the incredible industry, patience and self control that the really successful politician needs. His style of oratory belonged to the pre-microphone age. Perhaps he was never a Spurgeon, but in my heart of hearts I believe that had he been born thirty or so years earlier and followed the same career he might have achieved nearly as great a fame. As it was, like so many of his fellow ministers of all denominations he spent most of his life striving unavailingly against forces greater than the Devil, the forces of agnosticism and hedonism. He timed his entry on the religious stage badly.

Having lifted himself from the depth of the mine to the height of the pulpit he hoped to lift and push his son still higher. This was only partly ambition and partly due to the innate Welsh respect for the values of education. Like Mr. Wilson's father or Mr. Heath's he would have been proud and gratified to have had a son who was Prime Minister but he would have settled for an F. E. Smith. He saw the opportunity for a career in politics which opened up through the Bar and he began implanting the seed at an early age. Success at school was demanded. Extra coaching in the holidays was provided to a less than eager recipient. Scholarships had to be won to Mill Hill School and then to Oxford. After Oxford the bar and politics—this was the plan and very proud and happy was he when some of the steps on the ladder had been climbed. But long before he had died it was clear that his son would not be Prime Minister, or another F. E. Smith or even a moderately successful barrister and a back bench M.P. He may have been disappointed but he never showed it by the faintest sign of reproach or regret for what might have been.

After he died I came across some lines which he wrote at

Christmas in 1942. At the time his church at Clacton-on-Sea was non-existent, his home was bare of furniture, his wife was being bombed in London and his only son was somewhere in China. He was writing of his youth.

". . . hard were the days, unsure the rewards, the pit menacing their insecure lot who lusted for no rebuking gain, but, content to worship God. And give their sons a richer life, were happy though they be forgot . . ."

From the end of the Twenties onwards my father's material standard of living declined. Thanks to the sacrifices of my mother and father I have had the richer life—materially. I have gained the whole world and lost my soul.

Towards the end we avoided discussions on religion—we did not say that we would not discuss it but by mutual silent consent we did not touch it. Throughout the Nineteen Century Non-conformists struggled to get Oxford and Cambridge opened to their sons. They succeeded in 1871 and when I got to Mill Hill School I found there a grandson of one of the first to be allowed in, Nathaniel Micklem Q.C.— one of the only two men to be a Q.C. in the reign of Queen Victoria and Elizabeth II. But the success cost the Non-conformists dear. The sons who went to Oxford drifted away from the church of their fathers, drifted away to the Anglican church, to agnosticism, to indifference. At a time when the Establishment really meant something, the Non-conformists breached the walls of the Establishment and walked through the breach to become Conformists. The Mandarins of the Establishment, like the Mandarins of the old Chinese Empire, absorbed the barbarians who had broken through the Great Wall and began to civilise them—in the process softening their barbaric enthusiasm for anything, including religion.

The process which had been begun for me at Oxford reached its culmination when my mother was dying of cancer in a hospital in Blackburn. As she went over a period of months, weeks, days, shrivelling to a living version of the photos of Auschwitz, she never complained—but she did permit herself to say a few days before the end—"I hoped to go by now, but I think God must be cross with me wanting to go, so He's making me wait a little longer."

For all I know there may be a God—although I have never seen a satisfactory reconciliation between omnipotence and benevolence, no adequate explanation of why mortals should suffer as part of some divine experiment tortures, physical and mental, at least as bad as and often more prolonged than those man has inflicted on man. If indeed we are part of such an experiment and in order to grow in moral stature must pass through this vale of tears, choosing between good and evil, I can only say that I wish I had been asked whether I wished to take part in this trial or test, because in my heart I don't believe the whole of human history is worth the cry of one terrified child in the night; and if there is a God who could permit my mother in her death agonies to say what she said and kiss the hand of her Divine Torturer, I would like to see that God tormented with all the fires of Hell in which our ancestors so fervently believed.

But the cry will come, "God is a suffering God"—as man desperately tries to explain the inexplicable and reconcile the irreconcilable. He feels that he cannot attribute evil to God, and since he can no more explain the problem of pain than could Job, seeks to excuse God by limiting his omnipotence. But the trouble is that once you start talking about a God who is not omnipotent you start down a path which ends with a Bishop waffling meaninglessly about God as the ground of being. The hungry sheep look up and are not fed.

And so the churches continue to empty—not primarily because of the growth of materialism or through a lack of great preaching, or because Christianity is difficult to practise. It is because the church no longer seems to believe its own message, the message which gave the early martyr strength to die joyfully, the good news that Christ had risen from the dead. We weaker brethren accept that he suffered under

Pontius Pilate, that he was crucified, dead and buried but doubt that on the third day he rose again from the dead. Like Thomas, we demand more evidence. Seeing would be believing—if only we too could thrust our hands into his side. If it were true then indeed the Christian Church has a gospel to spread throughout the world. If it is not true then the Church has nothing more to offer than an interesting Jewish religious teacher of the first century, one of many which that amazing region has brought forth, one who in his own life opted out of most of the problems which confront the ordinary man, who has to do a soul destroying job while trying to raise a family.

For myself, like Henley, I feel that

"Beyond this place of wrath and tears

Looms but the horror of the shade"

but unlike him "the menace of the years" does not "find me unafraid." I can only go on and go out into the night hoping that I do not whimper too much at the end.

In the summer of 1958 my family was away on holiday. As I got out of the car I heard a 'phone ringing in the empty house. He was dead. He had collapsed at the top of the stairs on the way to bed. A few days later his funeral service was conducted by the Rev. Kenneth Dykes, the last Minister of Myrtle Street Baptist Church. My father belonged to that generation whose three score years and ten had encompassed more shattering changes than any other generation ever has or ever will—from the age of the horse to the threshold of moon travel through 'phones and wireless to television, from the last cavalry charge to the H-Bomb, from the British Empire at its height to the little England of the 1950s, from the accepted middle-class values and respectability of the Victorian Era to the sexual morals of today. The church was in decay, the dream of liberal progress had vanished in the millions dead in the world wars, the mass unemployment of the 30's, the gas ovens of Auschwitz, the concentration camps of Siberia and the starvation of most of mankind. He had seen

Non-conformity fall from being a powerful force in the nation whose leaders commanded respect and renown to being an irrelevance, an appendage of or hindrance to the Ecumenical Movement. His wife was dead; his son had failed to fulfil the great hopes placed in him; his congregation had melted away and his voice was a whisper. He to whom preaching was everything could no longer preach. But I do not think that he had lost his faith or his courage. As for the son—he can never go to church without weeping—weeping because there is inextricably intertwined the loss of a father with the loss of a faith, so that well-known and well-loved hymns give a double twist of the knife, so that any stumbling, doubting preacher recalls his father's towering presence and rock-like strength, a rock which has crumbled to dust and ashes.

Strong head, headstrong perhaps,
Hot tempered, lazy in some ways,
But strong in all moments of crisis
And in two tongues the true Celtic fire
Flamed through five thousand sermons
In fifty years of ugly chapels,
Crowded or empty, always giving his best.

And at the end,
That beautiful voice a whisper
He fought the spreading cancer for months,
Still valuing books and things that matter
And through the faith destroying pain
Did not curse God.

One night, he summoned all his strength,
To climb, alone, the narrow stairs to bed.
He reached the top and died.